The Artist Who *Thinks* Too Much

Rodney Chang

M.A., M.S.Ed., D.D.S., Ph.D.
M.A., M.A., M.A.
B.A., B.A.
A.A.

CREATIVE FRONTIERS INTERNATIONAL, INC.
HONOLULU, HAWAII

To order additional copies, please contact us.

Creative Frontiers International, Inc.
"www.PygoyaGallery.com"

Phone: 808-845-6216
Fax: 808-841-6872
Email: pygoya@hawaii.rr.com

Printed in the United States of America

FOREWARD

Dr. Rodney Chang, over a lifetime, has crossed many boundaries to deliver his unique vision in art. Not hung up like most about the political implications (such as threat to the established art market) of the digital medium that so profoundly transforms our life, Chang leaps forward to wean what he can out of the wired box, with the power to elicit an aesthetic response. Caring less about so-called "authorship," the artist embraces the role of psychologist and concocts his own "creative process" to produce his brand of art. "What you see is what you get" isn't necessarily true in his case. The artwork is merely the residue of a crucible that has been fired up, dissolving discipline boundaries in a fearless effort in order to personally exist in an experimental realm where *anything* can become *art* or aesthetic experience, as when the artist-psychologist-dentist converted his Honolulu dental clinic reception area into a discotheque (as reviewed on *Real People*, NBC, 1979-81). More sources of creative insight that can turn the banal into art includes what surfaces from his computer monitor, created sparks generated from his art theories, awareness on how we perceive art, and even peering with the eyes of the artist within the oral cavity.

This book is a collection of writings from the artist's decades-long diary. It documents chronologically where Chang's aesthetic interest lay at certain periods of his life as well as elucidates for us his journey as a developing digital (and multi-media) artist and Conceptualist. This publication becomes a history of one individual's journey as a pioneer of computer (or "digital") art from its humble PC beginnings. Through his own words the reader learns to appreciate Chang's profound passion and dedication for discovering new tools and methodology in order to manifest new vision for humanity now residing in the Information Age. A major concern of the artist is that our fine art keeps up with the rest of the evolving digital culture that continually shapes and enriches our daily life.

TABLE OF CONTENTS

Chronological List of essays in the artist's "Art Journal"

The Artist Who *Thinks* Too Much

Rodney E.J. Chang

M.A., M.S.Ed., D.D.S., Ph.D.
M.A., M.A., M.A.
B.A., B.A.
A.A.

Chronological entries in the artist's art diary

Unedited from the artist's diary.

The Future Mind and Art

Published in Mental Evolution and Art, Exposition Press, New York, NY, 1979

Interaction among time, environment, and species have led to an ascending order of mental complexity not only between genre, but also within the different species themselves. Thus the future man will be the product of the ongoing, accumulating new levels of consciousness designed to adapt to his ever-changing environmental demands. Extrasensory perception may be the first sign of another future common mental ability, or it may be a vestigial reminder of a once common ability of a distant ancestor. People often say, "Don't think too much!" because this not only can lead to the truth but also is dangerous because it leads to change – a thinking change that may be recorded genetically and thus permanently influence the essence of the human mind.

The future man will have a greater mental potential (relative to us) for responding to the challenges of his time. With the passage of thousands of years between kinfolk, a genetic gap develops and decreases mutual comprehension between people of different eras. Each era of man thinks differently and thus solves the problems of living in its own characteristic way.

The childhood of the future man's life will be relatively much longer than ours, and so probably will be the length of life. They'll have longer childhoods and the "kids" will possess larger brains. The contemporary man is evolving mentally along a direction of analytical thinking. Our fantasy levels keep us human as we are drawn relentlessly by the forces of cognitive and rational thinking abilities that create power and control over our environment and others. Maybe a million years from now man no longer will know "love," "emotion," or "war." He'll be the perfect living computer. But, as I said before, we all judge from a certain aesthetic bias that may be inappropriate to the other's preferred taste, that of the future mind.

As the landscape and architecture become more simplistically rectilinear, so do the art objects that combine with the interior forms of the architectural form. Art of the next century may focus on the environmental sensitivity that we are currently attempting to create in ourselves. And this developed sensitivity will be recorded and appreciated in the temples of our art. We may finally accept the fact that nature is the greatest artist. The nature of nature determined compositional rules. And nature, as artist often depart from the common drab of green trees and blue oceans, dresses up frequently into something more daring, such as the rainbow, the prism, the diamond, the neon tetra fish, the North Pole aurora, and the dazzling sunset. Maybe our future art will be more in tune and guidance with nature. It may change its cycles just like the seasons. Traditional rules for dividing art from the non-art of the world will break down. Anything can be viewed as art if the perceiver chooses to wear those particular lenses of interpretation. There will be a struggle between established art and anti-art guerrillas.

As man becomes more at home in the crowded urban metropolis, his art will change/evolve accordingly. New forms will emerge and be assimilated by the rest through the ball-carrying insight of that society's contemporary artistic geniuses. The new forms will emerge through the factories of crowd-taste guidance research. From all these new forms will follow the identity of the future changed world and a personal attachment to the specific time. And new products, packaged in the new taste extensions, make their way into the marketplace and under the Christmas tree. Artists, technicians, scientists, and philosophers will together determine future artistic growth and direction. Art will eventually marry technology so that each is indispensable to the other. The artist will no longer be just a craftsman but also a deliberate historian on his field of human thinking called aesthetics.

About ***Mental Evolution and Art***- *an innovative theory of human nature linking mental evolution with art as a catalytic force*
    – (A review)

Dr. Rodney Chang perceives evolution as a continuum not only of different physical species but also of mental levels of consciousness. Comparing the level of consciousness of a human when in deep sleep with that of the basal metabolism of plants, he asserts that "our minds are not just a polished and finished human product, but an amorphous entity of an infinite variety of thinking, all inherited from the potpourri of intelligent mechanisms adequate to support long past different ancestral forms of life." The conscious state, he theorizes, evolved more recently than the unconscious state. But if we accept the notion that thinking begins in an unconscious state, then perhaps "a sort of overall bio-mental energy system exists, forming a mental energy continuum related through evolution."

Man reacts to the chaotic world through his conscious state. By thinking, he creates an order that makes his world tolerable. Art is vital to human life for the psychological function it performs. Art objects are more than mere physical representations; they simulate different levels of consciousness to evoke emotional reactions and to help a person know himself better. By acting as such a stimulant, art provides a mental link to memories and fantasies, and it also prevents boredom.

An artist must create objects that strike a chord in the viewing public. An art object serves its purpose if it excites the viewer, making him more aware of himself.

Dr. Chang holds degrees in zoology (B.A., University of Hawaii-Manoa), psychology (B.A., Hawaii Pacific University), education (M.S.Ed., University of Southern California), art (M.A., Northern Illinois University), and dentistry (D.D.S., Loyola University, Chicago, IL)

Some Ideas of an Art Psychology

(Which help lead to the digital and cyberart of Pygoya)
By Rodney Chang, 1980*

1. Art is perceptual; it is psychological.

2. The power of aesthetic perception is the interaction between the object and the beholder.

3. The experimental aesthetic value of even the most successful art pieces is relative with changes in time and conditions of the society in which it resides.

4. Art, being psychological, includes both unconscious as well as conscious processes of the beholder. Developing this awareness and receptivity of the art object is called the sensitivity of the beholder.

5. Art stimulates more intensely than commonplace objects of the world through its inclusion of metaphorical discoveries left free for a multi-interpretive response by the beholder. In other words, ambiguity is a factor of aesthetic perceiving.

6. The results of aesthetic effort can be studied empirically (for example by social criticism or survey ratings) in order to help the artist refine and clarify his future work with more predictable audience reaction to his future efforts.

7. Art changes form as the times change. Today the strongest influence on our way of life and therefore art too is the accelerated advances of technology. Art can choose to cooperate with science in order to continue to be a viable vehicle for expanding our reality to keep up with the changing conditions of the world, and therefore life itself as we experience and perceive it.

8. Art therefore represents artifacts of past world realities and is a predictor of future changes of the evolving society, which lags behind the avant-garde in art in changing with the pressures of contemporary life.

9. The development of a feeling of integration and unity and the attempt to change or expand the reality of the times seems to be common problems and pursuits for artists across specific times and cultures.

10. An aesthetic model for relating the complex nature of the process of aesthetic perception can be heuristic in stimulating more new art.

11. Social, cultural, political, economic, and religious factors must be recognized in the perception of art, other than the readily visible qualities of the work of art.

12. There is a continuum of aesthetic perception, the best of which is given special reverence and identity as "art".

13. A systems approach is conceivable in explaining the process of art. Surely "art" includes biological and social learning that can be conceptualized into a "system" of aesthetics.

14. Because art is psychological, the choice of medium to trigger an aesthetic response is limitless.

15. Established cultural preferences are passed on, through formal education, to the young. Aesthetic values and judgments are developed as early as during the elementary years of schooling.

16. It takes both cerebral hemispheres to produce good art.

17. There is a trend today to de-emphasize the visible form that art takes with a corresponding elevation of the importance and appreciation of the message or idea (content) of the work of art.

18. Aesthetic appreciation can be fostered and discovered in real life situations instead of just within the limited context of art galleries and museums.

19. Situations, besides just objects, can elicit an intense aesthetic response that characterizes our feelings for the appreciation of the aesthetic in our life experience.

20. A developed model of aesthetics can lead to a parent world philosophy, for aesthetic perception is only a part of a broader phenomenon - the general psychology of man as it reflects his nature.

These conclusions by Rodney Chang (a.k.a. as Pygoya since 1987) are based on his doctoral study in aesthetics and the psychology of art at Union Institute, Cincinnati, Ohio from 1977 to 1980. Dr. Chang has used these tenants of an "art psychology" as a personal goal oriented philosophy in subsequent decades as a working artist. For example, dental materials are composed into mixed media sculptures and Asian utilitarian objects (such as sandals and chopsticks) melted and reformed in bronze. His dental clinic fascinated America when it was featured on national television because of a discotheque art installation that served as the "waiting room". He himself, became a walking art object as the "Disco Doc", a character intentionally developed after his health care project became notorious. Through past experience as a rock and roll band member and his love for dancing, "Disco Doc" improvised to discotheque crowds' delight, combining decades of styles seamlessly within a dance or two. Later life after disco led Dr. Chang into computers where with his mantra of art psychology he converted computer graphics to digital art. This feat early on in personal computer history is documented through solo museum exhibitions in the United States and abroad. With the advent of the Internet, Pygoya was among the first to transform digital art to "cyberart" then "webart" or "art made for contributing to the cyberculture of the online global community". To make that jump took conceptual decisions in regards to character, function, permanency of the works and of course perceived virtual audience needs and reactions. Today the movement of "Webism" is on firm footing, with artists around the world accepting its online manifesto (www.lastplace.com/webism.htm) and networking with Ingrid Kamerbeek of Germany, at http://www.artingrid.de/1sthourwebists1.htm

Dr. Rodney "Pygoya" Chang's Model of Aesthetics and Transformative Philosophy

1980

My model of aesthetics has been derived from over ten years of phenomenological searching for not just the real nature of art but also, as unconscious need for a personalized and clarified philosophy of art. One that integrates not only the divisions and compartments within the art world, but art with life itself. Thus I turned to personal experience and time to sort for a unifying sense of all my socially separated learnings and activities.

What does it all mean and what does it all add up for the meaning and quality of my life? Would each successive life situation and formal block of instruction in different fields add up to a rare realization that gains an overview of the contemporary reality (great insight through experienced perception)? Could I gain a greater "perceptual grasp" than most by doing more than is normal?

In mathematical form, the elements and their relationships are as such presented:

$$AA = r_o \left(\left[P + U + \frac{K_f}{K_d} + \frac{I_f}{I_d} \right]_o + r_a \left[\left(P + \frac{I_f}{I_d} + \frac{K_f}{K_d} \right) + G + M \right]_a \right)$$
$$\overline{\rule{0pt}{0pt}\hspace{3cm}}$$
$$t + m$$

Where,

AA= art appreciation
r_o= mental set or readiness of observer
r_a= mental set or readiness of artist
P = psychophysical stimuli and mental reactions
U = the Unconscious, including the irrational
K_f= knowledge of social origin that facilitates liking a specific something
K_d= knowledge of social origin that debilitates liking a specific something
I_f= Personal individual perceptual and Cognitive framework that facilitates liking something
I_d= Personal "preferences" that debilitate liking something
t = time
m = medium (-a) used
G = goal of the art work
M = material manipulation or transformation (technique)
o = observer's
a = artist's

Where,

AA = art appreciation or total perceptual response

r = attention, state of readiness or receptivity to perceive; mental set and mood

o = of observer

a = of artist

P = psychological elements

U = thought processes we are not aware of; i.e., the unconscious

K = cultural knowledge and standards

I = individual's personality and idiosyncratic aesthetic preferences

f = facilitates liking something

d = debilitates liking something

G = goal or intent of the artist's creative imagination

M = natural material manipulation to create psychological aesthetic stimulus

t = time passing

m = materials used, or medium (which can be completely conceptual and psychological)

My model is based upon a quantitative sizing up of the potentially aesthetic material in order to come up with an integrated personal interpretation that supports a judgment of quality of experience and encapturement of the feeling of the aesthetic or art. Like a computer our brains sum up an aesthetic situation,

subtracting the psychological turn-ons from the turn offs, in order to almost simultaneously determine the resultant intensity of
aesthetic quality felt from the stimulus. Much of the elements determining taste of course go on unconsciously and even automatically (one dogmatically rejects a certain brand of work or look).
One "knows" what one likes and dislikes.

My model takes into consideration the actual effect that politics, capitalism and industrialization, social aesthetic conditioning, the unconscious, and the personality of the spectator have on
the final "grasp" of the aesthetic stimulus perceptually. The physical constituent (for example the canvas and paints themselves) of
a work of art is thought of as just a stimulus for creative thinking
that is passed from artist to spectator.

Quality is influenced by time and fashion. Popularity of materials to work with varies with time and culture; goals for creating art change too. The aesthetic object or situation is the vehicle
for active communication of feelings and awareness between two
people, the artist and his public.

Norms come into play in the aesthetic experience by placing
brakes on too sudden changes in art. It's like a stabilizing factor of
the evolving art that is adapting to our new needs. Thus does my
model incorporate formistic thought. Just as my approach to isolating the spontaneous aesthetic perception (which leads to appreciation) is one of cumulating and summation, so is its nature quite
mechanistic as a view of human nature. Psychological elements are
definitely included, for the physiological sensations of art media
play excitatory and therefore sensuous roles for the aesthetic experience. The model is "hedonistic" in that it defines everything
that adds up (or subtracts from) to an aesthetic experience as "art
appreciation" or pleasurable.

Of course the model is highly organistic in nature, for it states
that larger entities, like art appreciation or aesthetic experience,
are the accumulation of other multi-level relationships of the human mind. The model points to the possibility of creating new
art with universal appeal; it serves as a tool to create art defended
by art criticism standards of the different world hypotheses. For
example, *Da Waiting Room* (dental discotheque office installation) is the aesthetic manifestation of 1) an individual's attempt
to make his environment and psychological space integrated and

thus reflect his personality to others, 2) the realization that the aesthetic experience can be found in real life situations besides traditional objects of art (contextualistic), and 3) everything in the world, including seemingly conflicting goals and situations, can be interrelated at a higher level of unified harmony, once creative insight and problems are worked out to mold the final aesthetic refinement of the work of art. The cited artwork challenges the norm of contemporary art, not to dethrone art but serve as catalyst for further growth and direction (real life situations) of this new form of art.

From such an eclectic (just like my "personality") model of aesthetic perception can be drawn a personal philosophy, an accidental award for the continued and disciplined study of art. I call it Transformative Philosophy. That's the fancy term that stands for a view of the world as one characterized by constant evolution through adaptive or maladaptive change, which at the same time maintains a constant relativity of all phenomena and things. Reality is relative, and so are facts. Evidence cannot pinpoint an ultimate reality but only support present or emerging hypotheses of these changing relationships of specific things tied to a high order of permanent unity. The wholeness of the universe is expressed as the final answer to personal conflict and aesthetic value. It is my duty to discern how all these different fields of study have interconnections that can be expressed aesthetically as a method of proving their existence. My art shall be based upon attention to change (in the world and in art) attached to a higher level of organization that maintains a sense of universal (or natural) unity among the artist, spectators and work of art.

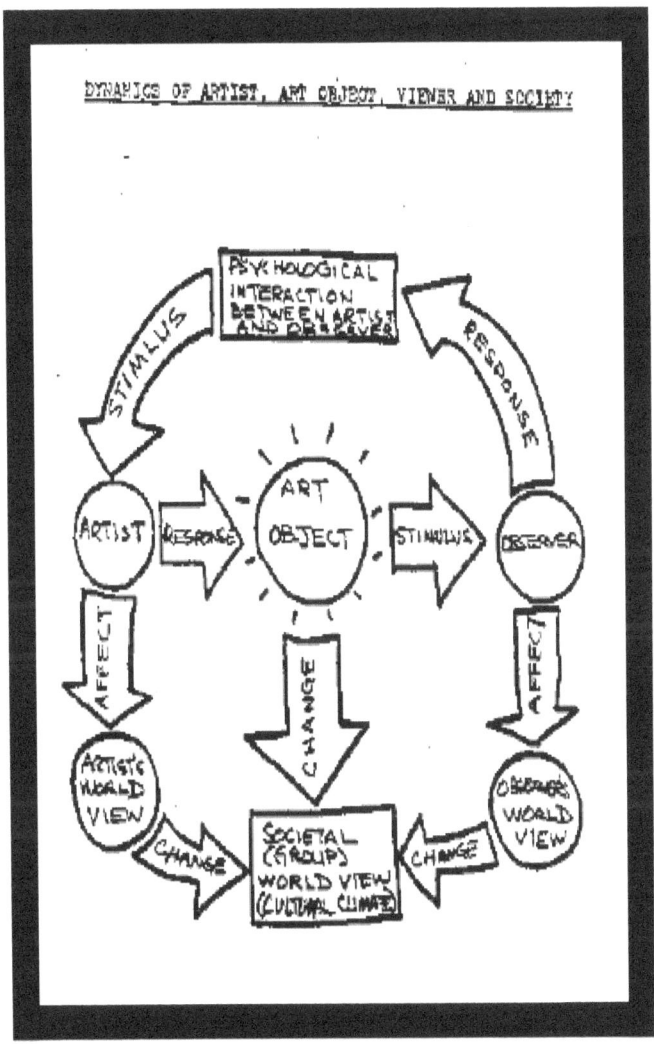

Dynamics of Artist, Art Object, Viewer, and Society
Rodney Chang, 1980

Philosophic Approaches to an Art Psychology

From Commentaries on the Psychology of Art, (unpublished)
Rodney Chang (1980)

Looking into the psychology of art I have touched upon the areas of intellectual thought of 1) psychology itself, especially perceptual and cognitive psychologies, 2) current aesthetic problems and concerns (i.e., the cutting edge of evolving art), 3) processes of creative thought and behavior, 4) phenomenological historical studies of past great artists, and 5) the aesthetic realm as differentiated from the non-art range of reality. Now I include still another important ingredient of art psychology, that of 6) philosophy. Indeed, art, or the aesthetic, is complex. Surely it extends beyond what the typical "art instructor" passes onto his student apprentices.

Why philosophy? Because one of my psychological art realizations is that ART IS PHILOSOPHICAL, besides psychological. That particular insight provided much understanding in regards to my questions on self-identity and behavior. Quite abnormal, I observe, for most professionals called dentists. Why my continued attempt to broaden my academic awareness and range of knowledge? Why my compulsion to know "what is art"? Why my lack of enthusiasm for traditional ways of learning and making art? Ultimately this all leads to the "Who am I?" - in order to adopt or develop an internalized philosophy of life that provides a rational interpretation of the facts of life that gives one not just reason and peace of mind but also purpose in life. In my lifetime, I had to gain, through personal effort, as good an understanding as anybody of the aesthetic. It just seemed the love for art was in my blood from birth. But it seemed to be limited by just what institutions taught students it could be. So I wandered into other pastures of study - biology, dentistry, education, psychology, and civics. Each remained more or less in its own academic world, staying within its own theoretical and categorical boundaries. Dentists learned only about teeth, artists taught good composition and how to mix paints, and psychologists trained to objectify their measurements of behavior. In fact so little cross-exchange goes on that friends wondered and warned of the cumulative effect on one brain! I must admit I've had my fears too - as to what would become of this fragmentary accumulation of information and ultimately ME!

Attempting to design some alternative education for myself was not easy. Art is right brain. Psychology is left. Now try to convince a traditional institution of higher education to grant you a degree in Art Psychology. Some administrator may wonder, "How can intuition and taste be compatible with statistical treatment of science?" Such lack of comprehension, at the highest intellectual level, provides evidence of the state of fragmentation and separation of our current knowledge of the world.

I did find myself become less enthusiastic about my field of interest when I tried, as scientific researcher, to chop up "art" into a cut and dry factor analysis. Art has always been somewhat magical or mystical - I had to at least be sure to maintain the <u>unconscious</u> or <u>irrational</u> in any derived equation of art appreciation or response. But yet the demands of a Ph.D. in "psychology" required an adherence to strict quantitative and traditional scientific modes of investigation.

Then it dawned upon me that all of the above has to do with a less rigorous discipline - philosophy. Everything cannot be measured in the realm of philosophy but can still be truths and values. For example, an explanation and interpretation of an aesthetic model or theory. The model can be tested by empirical experimentation for validity, but also through compatibility and extension of a school of philosophy. If one adopts a mechanistic philosophy to interpret the data and facts available in order to construct a reality (a system of understanding and beliefs of the causation of phenomena), then he can easily accept a mechanistic aesthetic model with which to judge art. Philosophy provides alternative ways of interpreting the facts of experimentation. Opposing camps in any field sprout up because facts are valid when they support the respective opponents' theoretical models. In other words, philosophy points out that there can be different truths derived from facts about phenomena, truths that are declared because they are compatible with a particular philosophical belief or worldview. Perspective plays a role in how we perceive or derive "facts".

So it seemed that turning towards philosophy might provide some understanding of my most unusual life. It seems that my quest for understanding of different fields of study stems from an inner frustration and realization of a "division of labor" mentality of organized higher education - at the expense of not providing a more liberal art approach to education and ultimately life itself. I now see each degree earned as a fragment of information that show how everything fits into a larger whole and awareness, one based upon My broad but specific interests. Why can't a dentist also be an artist? I am not there yet, but this phenomenological approach to study promises to bear fruit.

I can also see now why there's a problem with an "Art Psychology". Much of my problem in studying the aesthetic has been in feeling forced to convert art into statistics. But now I know that the study of art psychology can also include feelings and belief/assumptions and still be objective.

Philosophy provides alternative realities by which to create scientific questions about the nature of these dissimilar realities. Research works out the details of proposed alternative world philosophies/realities/hypotheses about life and existence. During my tenure as a student of aesthetics I now see the strength of my results to be dualistic in character at different levels of interpretation. At the lower level, art provides me a therapeutic way to treat dental patients with less anxiety on both sides. At a higher level, my art is integrated into an internalized view of the world, a philosophy. With an overriding philosophical point of view, my facts of art psychology would be "scattered" and thereby less meaningful. In art one can be loose and relaxed enough to draw from unknowns in order to create new things or awareness. However, this mixture of the irrational with the analytical does not block the ability to look at art critically and objectively. If a process, although some of its elements may be less than "scientific", produces new art, at predictable levels, then it becomes a legitimate *modus operandi* for human progress.

What follows is a detailed commentary by me on the important ideas by Stephen C. Pepper in The Basis of Criticism in the Arts that are relevant to art psychology. Dr. Pepper presents four major different world philosophies, or "world hypotheses" as he refers to them, and from such independent stands then de-

fines what the "aesthetic" is, as logical extensions of these alternative philosophies. I will use my art environment/happening, "Da
Waiting Room," as an art illustration when making comments on
Pepper's ideas and lastly, compare and contrast my own model
of aesthetic perception with the models of aesthetics proposed by
these different world hypotheses.

INTRODUCTION

Pepper (from here on, "P" for Pepper): All that philosophy
does is to see to it that all the relevant facts are brought into consideration ... Dogmatism - an attitude of belief (or disbelief) in
excess of the grounds of belief (or disbelief)... The great breeding
ground of dogmatism today is the appeal to certainty... Multipli-
cative corroborations give us the kind of facts which we associate
with physics and with the sciences generally... it is the corroborations that comes from taking an observation repeatedly...till we are
quite sure there has been no error....It is the corroboration of one
observation with another, or of one man with another.... Facts so
corroborated were called data... Structural corroboration requires
a hypothesis to indicate the way in which the evidence may con-
verge to corroborate a fact. The hypothesis holds all the corrobo-
rating facts together in a system and, in so far as the hypothesis is
verified, the whole system of facts gains in probability.... In tracing
the main evidential support of (art) criticism to structural corroboration, and hence finding that we are thereby led to world
hypotheses, we discover that criticism is philosophical in its foun-
dations. Sound criticism is the application of a sound philosophy
to works of art ... A sound philosophy is an empirical one, nothing
more than as complete a systematization of the world's evidence as
can be made, nothing more than a world hypothesis describing the
structural lines of corroboration of evidence. In applying world
hypotheses to the problem of criticism we are simply making use
of all the evidence available, so that our judgments may have the
widest possible empirical base.... But in world hypotheses it appeared that there are a number of alternative ways of organizing
the world's evidence; that is, that there are a number of alternative
world hypotheses. The main ones are called formism, mechanism,
contextualism, and organicism. None is completely corroborated

by its evidence, so that we cannot accept any of them as an entirely true or adequate description of our world. We might regard them as four different approximations to the nature of the world. They are cornering it, so to speak, from different sides. Since they all seem to be about equally adequate we cannot dispense with any of them until a definitely superior hypothesis should appear... The four alternative relatively adequate world hypotheses represent simply the best organizations of evidence achieved up to the present time, and consequently the best knowledge of art at our disposal... we are on our guard against types of criteria (in criticism of art) that rest their claims on common sense and the closely allied appeals to certainty and self-evidence and tradition and other ways of taking things for granted, and against those that rest their claims on authority not backed by evidence, and those that rest on animism and mysticism, which are very inadequate world hypotheses... It follows that good criticism is, ... criticism based on a good philosophy. For a good philosophy is simply the best disposition of all evidence available... A thoroughly competent critic is one who has both intimate experience with the art he is judging and possession of reliable criteria of criticism.

So here is presented Pepper's view of art criticism. It is the best interpretation of a work of art available to the expert; one's whose judgment is based upon an empirical philosophy derived from an operational systematization of the facts of worldly observations. It makes good sense that "art appreciation" should be an extension of our mental selves and our perceived relation to the world. Art is a product of the psychology and philosophy of man. As such art is rooted in "real life," and as such, can be observed empirically for better understanding of the hidden processes of aesthetic experience. People's responses and feelings towards a work of art can be added up into some sort of cumulative prediction of future behavior affect by the same work of art on future spectators. Art can be studied like another field of psychology. The effect of art on people can be measured and predicted. Now Dr. Pepper presents-

A Theory of Empirical Criticism

P: ... human preferences are facts ... have a firm basis in the structures of human behavior and the human mind. .... there is emphatic need for the evidence of the nature of the mind, since the aesthetic experience draws heavily on emotion, memory, perception, imagination, and, in fact, on every major topic of psychological investigation.

RC: Thus I, as an art graduate student of painting and drawing, left at a loss in my search for the meaning of art, when I completed the traditional program leading to the Masters of Art at a state university. It was only natural that I should turn to psychology, a department outside of the fine arts, in order to find out for myself what the art professors were not teaching or did not know. Once I brought some books on aesthetic theory to class. My professor of painting said they looked interesting but "if time was spent reading all that material, when would there be time for painting?"

P: History, anthropology, social theory, physics, psychology, and really also biology are all involved.

RC: I would say my natural impulse is towards art and creativity. Thus intuitively it may have been that I was attracted to study other fields outside of art in order to get a better grasp of the true nature of art. I think everything, every field, is involved in "art." At the lowest level, every field of human activity requires good design for its equipment and work situation. At the higher level art can be an ideal set for the desires for further growth and development of the specific fields.

P: You might think that it would require a superman to bring the results of all our knowledge to bear on the objects of a special field... the structure of knowledge as a whole has been a human interest for many centuries... called philosophies... better called world hypotheses ... comprehensive understanding a major pursuit.

RC: Is that what has been driving me? The search for a personal philosophy not just for art but also towards life?

P: The big issues over the nature of knowledge and the organization of evidence go on between the schools, between the integral world hypotheses. If, then, anyone wants to apply the whole weight of our knowledge to any specific field, the way he can do this is to direct these world hypotheses upon the subject matter of his field and see what the results are.

RC: I intend to use my tools of art psychology to interpret the living condition and problems of different fields normally without any fine arts representation. (Computer graphics, 1985-; Internet cyberculture, 1997-; sci-fi writings integrating UFO phenomena and fine arts, 2005-)

P: My position is that there is a preponderance of evidence for connections for fact in nature but that the precise manner of the connections is open to hypothesis.

RC: A better chance to fabricate a valid hypothesis about the facts of nature is by taking a sampling of them from different areas of study, to detect and cast out the built-in biases (intellectually and occupationally) of the different built-in value systems of each field or occupation. By such an eclectic education matrix can one see facts of different fields, isolated from each other, in a broader light. One can start to search for an overall explanation or philosophy of the "connections" among facts with more objectivity than that of a strict specialist of information. Wisdom is nurtured when we look for universality that lies beyond the obvious facts.

P: (Art) judgments are applications of one or another definition of the aesthetic field held by the critic, and the empirical legitimacy of these judgments depends on the empirical justification of the definition... It has rather recently been discovered that definitions are the ultimate basis of judgments of value ... We now clearly see that the basis of the whole matter is a definition.

RC: yes, what is "art?" What makes the "eyes" different for each beholder?

P: It is essential that a definition employed as a criterion of value ... should contain a truth reference... should be responsible to the relevant facts ... responsible to the facts and empirically secure ... Otherwise, the definition would be completely arbitrary and irresponsible and totally unfit for its function as a basic criterion on value ... (must) frame a descriptive definition of the aesthetic field for each world hypothesis. This is the fundamental criterion of aesthetic judgment for the view concerned. This gives us a qualitative judgment for what is or is not aesthetic. Quantitative standards are directly developed out of this definitional criterion by noting what quantitative factors there are among the characters of the definition, which describe the aesthetic field. Since these standards are derived from a description of the relevant facts, these standards are as firmly based empirically as the definition itself.

RC: And thus Pepper brings aesthetic judgment or criticism and appreciation into the realm of science. An approach for art psychology, although science is not the only one (for example, the use of inspiration to solve artistic problems).

RC: Aesthetic perception is what art is. What we like is the "quality" of things; the most intensely being works of art. If enough people have the same preference (although preference can be fostered from a multitude of psychological reasons), it becomes a statistic or datum that can be defined or described. Thus what the norm likes becomes the "standard." Standards thereby eventually remain standards for other than the original aesthetic change (or evolve), or as people change their relative sense of quality for things, so will the numbers change in describing the new aesthetic situation or social aesthetic perception.

MECHANISTIC CRITICISM

P: That pleasure is good and pain is bad is generally taken as fact not to be doubted without ridicule, so evident as to need no further evidence. On this datum the mechanistic theory of criticism is based.

RC: Also called the hedonistic theory of aesthetics.

P: The universe is conceived as a huge aggregation or system of essentially separate individuals. ... The higher-level entities are described as combinations of lower level entities, but the entities on any one level are separate entities with their own locations in the space-time field and their own autonomy. Even atoms have movement.

RC: In such a way can the elements of composition be viewed as autonomous entities but tied together in some sort of balanced equilibrium by the skills of the artist.

P: Definition of the aesthetic field is then that of objectified pleasure. ... the aesthetic field as that of completely absorbed pleasant experiences. ... This .. is a description of fact. It is as fully empirical as possible with the data available. It is tied in with, and has the corroboration of a great mass of empirical description from psychology, biology, and physics.

RC: Thus the mechanistic model calls "art" a pleasurable experience, i.e., psychological.

P: Things liked or disliked for themselves would thus be the field of aesthetic values and the values would lie in the feelings of pleasure and displeasure... Aesthetic value is defined as feelings of immediate pleasure and displeasure, whence objects of aesthetic value are objects that produce or attract these feelings, then for the hedonic view this definition becomes the basic qualitative criterion of aesthetic judgment.

RC: I wish there isn't the negative connotation of being hedonistic. Doesn't everyone, in fact, seek the good life and seek pleasure instead of pain? Isn't achieving happiness pleasure seeking? Why be jealous of others' achieved level of happiness?

P: The more of immediate pleasure in an experience the greater the aesthetic value, and a great work of art is one that can be relied upon to produce a great deal of pleasure.

RC: Like a good-looking lover.

P: ... since pleasures received from objects vary with the person and his mood or physiological state, it follows that all elementary aesthetic judgments in the form "This gives me such an amount of immediate pleasure" are relative .... It is unmeaning to say that what is beautiful to one man ought to be beautiful to another.

RC: This is the theory of beauty "is in the eyes of the beholder."

P: Every judgment supported by evidence of introspective report or external observation that "this gives immediate pleasure to so and so" is an objective statement ... And as for general assertions, every work of art designed to appeal to a certain public is in the nature of a prediction that members of this public will derive immediate pleasure from that object. These predictions are verified often enough to provide a great mass of material for systematic general aesthetics. The bases of these generalizations are the essential biological similarity of human organisms, the similarity of their capacities for intellectual, emotional, and sensory development, and the similarity of reaction induced by identical cultural surroundings.

RC: This is what my book, <u>Mental Evolution and Art</u> says about aesthetic perception. It's more than psychological - it's tied to our evolutionary biological selves.

P: "It is unintelligent not to get the greatest pleasure out of life that life can give. In this we discover a certain obligation to ourselves, one that has its roots within ourselves.

RC: Agreed.

P: -hedonic standard of beauty: the emergence of a general obligation to refine our senses so as to obtain the most pleasure of which our bodies are capable ... the genius of hedonic criticism lies in its sensuous discrimination.

P: Actually the judgment of the capacity of a work of art to give pleasure is perfectly objective. When the relevant variables are put in, such as the degree of an individual's hedonic discriminations and the influences of his cultural environment, the judgment is not only objective but also stable and a sound basis for prediction. ... a work of art of great aesthetic value is one that affords a great deal of immediate pleasure to a highly discriminatory taste.

RC: - the art critic.

P: Santayana writes, "Nothing has less to do with the real merit of a work of imagination than the capacity of all men to appreciate it; the true test is the degree and kind of satisfaction it can give him who appreciates it most."

RC: This places the most power aesthetically with the professional critic. There is no other competing standard of beauty other than himself. The sanctioned "discriminating expert is the concrete embodiment of the hedonic standard."

RC: Upon the hedonic standard of aesthetics could I defend the quality of art of Da Waiting Room. I consider myself the best judge of the aesthetic content and quality of the work, with full understanding of how I, as the artist, conceived it as art, not merely dental clinic space. Da Waiting Room is art dependent upon eliciting the feelings of pleasure - through the space's interior decorating, hung art, and disco music, while playing with the cultural limitations of isolated situational perception (usually a disco and dental office are visually and therefore conceptually separated and thereby deemed incompatible). Da Waiting Room aesthetic question to its recipients of pleasurable feelings is this - if we, through "common sense," eliminate the possibility of the coexistence and integration of disco dentistry, how probably is it that mental limitations of other elements of our varied environment restrict our visual and experiential "reality?" Through the manipulated juxtapositions the different elements of eliciting pleasure (disco being the standard of audio pleasure here) are tied together by the mental experiencing of its intended population (patients, staff and the community in general) for identify as a larger aesthetic whole than any of its pleasure-evoking constituent parts (including my hung paintings). Being the only expert on the art project for eighteen months, I consider myself the best critic of the "work of art." I know it is "read" as "art" by several ways: by comments like "I really like being in this place but don't know why" (it's abstract to him but he can sense pleasantness from it) and large happy eyeballs of exploratory children waiting their turn for dental treatment in the dazzle of pleasurable sounds and sights.

I believe there is more to "art" than the feelings of pleasure derived from the senses. This will all be brought out - the similarities and differences of this and the following three world hypotheses derived aesthetic hypotheses with later discussion of my own "model of aesthetic perception." The latter of which has been formulated through phenomenological study and participation with conceptual art projects such as "Da Waiting Room" and "Marine's Window." Notice that this world hypothesis does not place innate aesthetic value in objects but see aesthetic quality as projections of the human mind that produce pleasure. From the hedonic perspective, a work of art or art per se is psychological.

CONTEXTUALISTIC CRITICISM

P: The basic concept of contextualism is a context of activity.
RC: "Da Waiting Room!"
P: Contextualism is the youngest of the relatively adequate worldviews and is still in its tentative stages.
RC: So is its art derivatives like happenings, installations and Da Waiting Room.
P: A situation includes both agents and circumstances, so action and the situation go together. The agent is faced by circumstances within the situation, and the act is his response to the problem they present. Through it the total situation, including both agent and circumstances, is changed in some way. ... The situation is one. It is a natural fact with a natural unity, not a construct made and existing only in the mind. ... It is not an assemblage of people, things, events, qualities and relations, pleasures, pains, and interests, combined in and by the perspective of some given indi-

vidual (Disco Doc). All these are among its constituents, but it is itself an independent unit (aesthetic unit). Its unity is constituted by a characteristic quality, which is unique in each situation.

RC: Apply all of the above to Da Waiting Room - it is "art."

P: We are always acting within a limited setting that includes various circumstances, and probably other actors in addition to ourselves. In this sense the situation, including both agent or agents and the circumstances confronting him or them, is the unit of experience. Moreover, it has value quality, as is suggested by such descriptive words as those above: cheerful, dynamic, and hostile.

Aesthetic experience is obviously to be found, on such a view, in the human situation... the contextualistic definition of the aesthetic field: voluntary vivid intuitions of quality. ... The more vivid the experience and the more extensive and rich its quality, the greater its aesthetic value ... Value lies in the situation as a whole, and the aesthetic value lies in the intensity and extensity of its quality.

RC: Da Waiting Room is quite a vivid experience to go through as a patient. If the curiosity or even ambiguity of environmental space doesn't get you, the colorful and energetic artwork will - or just the loud pulsating disco music.

P: Intensity and depth of experience - that is the contextualistic standard of beauty.

RC: The longer I experience Da Waiting Room the more intense the aesthetic experience becomes. Of course I have become fatigued by the outer visual shell (the physical elements of composition of the space) but the conceptual content continues to intensify my spirit through growing identity and attachment to the aesthetic statement and the rekindled first impression/reaction through empathy with the day's new patient's appreciation of the space.

P: For it is the quality that determines the unity and range of a situation (at least aesthetically) and it is the fused details and relations that determine the content. There is accordingly no sharp line in experience between the aesthetic and the nonaesthetic. Aesthetic value runs out into all life...

RC: Da Waiting Room (1997: also surfing the Internet environment plus entering into a virtual online museum plus viewing cyberart in a vrml context)

P: The normal structure of a mechanistic book of aesthetics is from the elements to the wholes; that of a contextualistic book from the wholes to the details... handling of conflict for aesthetic purposes is a peculiar contribution of contextualism.

RC: Yes, in any art project the artist works both ways - with particulars that will add up to the whole effect and with the overall concept or purpose of the work of art before getting on with the actual fabrication of the piece.

P: So far as art depends on culture and not upon instinct, the art of one age cannot be vividly repeated in another... critics are required in each age to register the aesthetic judgments of that age.

P: The perception of a work of art is clearly the awareness of the quality of the situation.

P: Strictly speaking, the quality of the picture is only realized on the occasions when it is actually perceived. Each such experience is an aesthetic experience ("art" occurs).

RC: This is exactly what I wrote in <u>Mental Evolution and Art.</u>

P: -the aesthetic work of art is the cumulative succession of intermittent perceptions. It is $P1 + P2 + P3$... The aesthetic work of art is not continuous but intermittent. ... the potentiality of the cumulative series of perceptions and of the ideal of the fully realized and funded perception at the end of the series lies in the actual continuity of the physical work of art.

RC: Every day that I return to work I receive another $Pn + 1$ to my cumulative perception and experience of Da Waiting Room. Monotony must be counterbalanced by contextual richness and empathic experience by daily new patients (fresh initial preceivers).

P: - a new function for the critic: contribute as far as he can to the complete realization of great works of art. ... It is an act of producing the values latent therein.

RC: And so I keep writing and teaching about The Waiting Room.

ORGANISTIC CRITICISM

P: Organicism, traditionally known as objective idealism, is

the world hypothesis that stresses the internal relatedness or co-
herence of things ... -observation at first apparently unconnected
turn out to be closed related, and with the fact that as knowledge
progresses it becomes more systematized... Value in the sphere of
knowledge is integration of judgments; in the sphere of ethics, it
is integration of judgments; in the sphere of art, it is integration of
feelings. ....Finally, it conceives all of these as contained in a total
integration of existence or reality.

RC: Thus by paying attention to any one aspect of the above,
like the sphere of art, one can hope to discover other higher level
connections of reality and gain a more integrated sense of existence.

P: Like contextualism, it is not impressed with the apparent boundaries of men's bodies (like the mechanistic hypothesis).
It deals with situations, but regards a contextualistic situation as
merely a way station to a larger integration.

RC: Thus organistic thought goes beyond the Ying-Yang dichotomy and the acceptance of mutual equality of the different
major world hypotheses. Everything culminates into an absolute
unified whole; if one looks long enough one can find interrela-
tionships between/among things. Disco-dentistry, art psychology,
work-play interaction and dental art are just a few examples of
how I am developing understanding and applications of higher
integrations of specific knowledges.

P: To reach the organistic idea, one is not far off if he starts
with the vivid situation of the contextualist and instead of stress-
ing the quality and defining the unity of the situation by the quality, stresses the organization and defines the unity of the situation
in terms of its organization .... Organistic definition of aesthetic
value: the integration of feeling.

RC: Organistic thought is similar to Buddhist ideas of a unity
of the universe. Thus a painting ought to, by organistic criticism,
bring about a deep and profound feeling of integration in the observer of the work of art.

P: The organicist is not much concerned about defining feeling precisely, because in the higher integrations it merges with the
ethical and logical connections anyway.

L: If disco and dentistry are not kept separate entities in the
mind, through constant repetitive physical correlation together,

such as The Waiting Room, they become associated and eventually become a new situation that is more than just a dental office and discotheque added together.

P: The aesthetic field is really defined by its origins among pleasures and the kind of connections indigenous to these origins rather than by any special sort of subject matter.

RC: Da Waiting Room becomes aesthetic because of the inclusion of the pleasant origins of disco, dance and the unpleasant origins of dental treatment. Together they blend into a new perception of receiving the treatment in a more humane and tolerable manner, characterized by less feelings of anxiety and elements of actual pleasure.

P: It takes imagination, we say, to feel them (connections) out. And here we come upon the organicist's special use of the term "imagination." .... It is the process of following out and building up feeling connections. With this in mind, another definition of aesthetic value for an organicist could be "imaginative integration."

RC: Teachings derived from Da Waiting Room.

P: Aesthetic material is not just what the eye and the ear respond to but also the images and meanings and emotions below the sensory surface. Anything that begets a feeling connection is aesthetic material. And ultimately there is probably nothing that may not be drawn into an aesthetic integration. Politics and business, medicine (dentistry), factory labor, (disco)...

RC: It's my hope that the supreme use of my knowledge of the psychology of art is to achieve the ability to do the "ultimate" Pepper speaks above of.

P: When it is necessary to ask an artist what he was trying to do, either the spectator or the artist is weak... In the hands of a competent artist a work of art makes itself, so to speak, and the further it gets along the more nearly it does so literally....(computer automatic image processing experimentation by Chang, 1990s)

RC: **I guess this means too that in abstract art, the ability of the artist to induce the spectator to recognize the material "below the sensory surface" is a creative responsibility that serves as a criterion for success and attainment of aesthetic value.**

P: -demands of feeling in aesthetic materials, bringing into the work materials called for by other materials till a complete organic unity is established. Then the work stops of itself, is self-explanatory, and objective.

RC: Each side of Da Waiting Room, i.e., the disco and the dental treatment areas, suggested alternative successive visual changes in the overall environment. For example, visual observation of the dancers required a see-through glass wall from the dental chairs, and the loud party volume disco required a separate volume control for chair-side dental relaxation to the same music.

P: An understanding spectator is a critic, and a critic is simply an understanding spectator who is perhaps a little more articulate in communicating the experience he has in a work of art ... Even the difference between artist and spectator is partially broken down on this view. ... The artist creates, the spectator recreates.

RC: This is almost exactly the way I describe the creative connection between artist and spectator in <u>Mental Evolution and Art</u>. Except I said that the artist creates the imaginative stimulus and the spectator continues the aesthetic power of the object by using his creative interaction with the piece for the sake of developing art appreciation feelings.

P: When the spectator is dissatisfied, then the question is whether the spectator or the artist is wrong in his imaginative construction.

RC: Both are creators, but either the work doesn't possess aesthetic quality integration or the spectator is not sensitive enough to be aware of the integration bestowed before him.

P: If the "literary" (psychological) values integrate in their feeling references with the plastic (materialistic) values, or vice versa, they are intrinsic materials of the work of art.

RC: I use the dental situation as a base from which to derive a special aesthetic value - application of aesthetic theory to dental work.

P: -sensations, images, thoughts, and emotions seek to come together of their own accord about a perceptive center such as a physical work of art.

RC: The Waiting Room is the "perceptive center", not the shot and drill.

P: It joins artist, critic, and spectator, or all who seek aesthetic values, into a community united in the creation of objects (or situations) of the highest aesthetic worth.

RC: some patients will never understand Da Waiting Room because they are just there for the dental treatment. They don't know or care "beans" about art. Life is too demanding for many of them to have the opportunity to focus on that aspect of life. They're too realistic about their life's limitations. On the other hand, many art critics would turn down an invitation to come and experience the environmental space, because to them, it's outside the realm of the fine arts. Too bad these have not acquired a higher integration of aesthetic sense and purpose.

FORMISTIC CRITICISM

P: Formism, ... stresses the fact of the normal, seeks to isolate it, and to define value in terms of it.

RC: This contributes validity to the ways of the "art establishment" but puts down avant-garde expressions of the aesthetic. Maybe this is why progressive artists remain reactionary and rebellious towards anything that becomes established as the standards of good art.

P: From psychiatry and particularly from psychoanalysis studies we are gradually acquiring a pretty clear picture of the nature and development of a normal personality (normal?) and of the structure of human values connected with it.

RC: Including aesthetic values, of course. I disagree that psychiatry and psychoanalysis provide good norms from which to derive a normative aesthetic. I prefer to investigate the aesthetic of Rogerian humanistic counseling, one based on successful empathic relationships for success in therapy.

P: States of equilibrium are discontinuous in nature, and extend up through all the levels of natural integration... - the picture takes on an appearance of continuity and the state of relatively stable equilibrium becomes a region of slightly varying structures of varying stability rather than a point of one fixed stable structure.

RC: Of course this is contrary to organistic aesthetic thought.

P: The significance of such evolutionary factors as the survival of the fittest now begins to be seen.

RC: Yes, art also evolves and the predominating art style of a moment is the "survival of the fittest" that is contemporary in social recognition.

P: - a norm of the species becomes a norm of value.

RC: What this theory does not take into account is the influence of change. Norms must always continue to evolve in order to keep up with our ever-changing and adapting selves. Norms in the aesthetic too must continue to evolve and remain vital or else die off and make room for a new breed and generation of art.

P: In short, defining value in terms of a natural norm is as justifiable as defining it in terms of satisfaction of interest.

P: In the end nature always takes the man's place in determining norms of adjustment.... This observation is the great contribution of formism, which has a pervasive though often hidden bearing on every aspect of human life including the aesthetic.

RC: And in the end nature determines the evolution of our art, since it is determined by the normative functioning of our biological, including the physical and mental, selves, which, in turn, enables us to adjust to the art of the times which not only reflects the present quality of life but also reality. Thus do we adapt, as an organism, to our evolving aesthetic.

P: My hypothesis on formistic evidence is that certain types of social equilibrium can be developed out of organisms that as individuals would be considered relatively unstable.

RC: Ah, the Disco Doc and Da Waiting Room.

P: Aesthetic value has been defined as conformity with the norm implicit in the art object itself.

RC: Ah, the vested interest of commercial galleries to keep what wells good at the top of the market. New art is threatening to the established business of art. That is why, maybe, the artist seeking change (dedicated artistic effort) is always characterized as one that is "starving."

P: Definition - perceptions satisfying in themselves to the normal man. ...-a normal man finds satisfaction in the representation of the traits and the actions of normal men. There is an ancient theory of perception, older even than Aristotle, which states that only like perceives like ... A man appreciates in that only a normal man, with a well integrated and relatively free emotional life, can perceive normality.

RC: That sounds as if the normal man on the street is a better critic of art than the artist burdened with the heavy emotions of existence.

P: The norm is embodied there (in the work), and a normal man finds satisfaction because his impulses are in harmony with the impulses of the work, both being normal.

RC: This hypothesis embeds the work of art with its own emitting aesthetic quality. Both art appreciation and perception of the spectator and the work of art are separate entities that are harmonious with the natural norms of nature.

RC: Good art always is ambiguous with the compositional (visually and psychologically) quality mixed in together with an air of instability (constant shifts in the equilibrium of nature and therefore also "art' as contemporaries appreciate it).

P: Formism in its stress on the perceptions and reactions of the normal man thus acts as a sort of governor over the whole aesthetic field. It holds art to the healthy golden mean, to what is sane and sound.

RC: This is my least preferred world hypothesis; it cramps innovative creativity and places an authority (the norm of a society, which can be manipulated or consciously developed by those with the power, such as that of mass media advertising or political propaganda objective) as the absolute judge of aesthetic quality and value of the art work produced during a period.

P: Art here more than expresses or represents the norm. It has insight into man's emotional requirements and actively returns him to the norm.

RC: That's why original artists reject the past and its artistic masterpieces, each deriving its stature by the aesthetic norms of the period. Because art fulfills "emotional requirements," under this theory of art and reality, all art is therapeutic.

P: -the critic's aesthetic aim is to bring these all together in a judgment of the effectiveness and worth of the work of art in establishing emotional balance and in attaining for the individual the satisfaction of normality.

HOW THE FOUR TYPES OF CRITERIA OPERATE TOGETHER

P: Judgment of the Mechanist: pleasures of the senses .. such as sound (disco for me!) and in the pulse of rhythm (fixing teeth to disco background tempo for me) ... pleasures of association ... pleasures of design .... pleasures of pattern ... pleasures of recognition or of the fulfillment of type ... sensations, images, design, pattern, and type - these are the principle sources of aesthetic delight.

P: Judgment of the Organicist: highly integrated and richness of a bundle of material expressing the interconnectedness of things and reality.

P: Judgment of the Contextualist: a splendid harmony of cumulative (perceptions) ... (aesthetic feelings from the situation).

P: Judgment of the Formist: ... induces balance and adjustment of character in the (spectator) reader.

P: A critic cannot say ahead how the views will combine or diverge in judgment on a specific work. In short, these philosophical views really do draw the aesthetic values out of the works of art and into the open.

RC: Here the author suggests a serially dissection and analysis of a work of art from the different world hypotheses viewpoints of reality. This sounds piecemeal to me - like the search goes on to provide a more all-encompassing and parsimonious view of everything at the same supreme plane of systematic organization, in order to give reality a broader awareness and actualization.

P: (the eclectic definition of aesthetic response framed by the author)- "An experience of beauty is one vivid in quality (contextualistic), highly organized (organistic), and a source of immediate enjoyment (mechanistic) for a normal mind (formistic)," or "an object of beauty is a normal perceptual integration of feelings highly pleasant (mechanistic/formistic/organistic), and vivid in quality (contextualistic)."

RC: I will compare this level of integration with that of my own proposed model (and therefore world hypothesis) of aesthetic perception (or psychology) later.

P: By the method we have followed (taking each point of view in turn and accepting the completely worked out judgments as a group) we can have both rational clarity in criticism (and art appreciation - Chang) and the reasonableness of wisdom (right brain integrated with left brain).

RC: All that is necessary to realize is that **facts are relative to the belief system it extends or clarifies. This orientation brings art into the realm of empirical psychological investigation.**

P: In practical criticism, a critic is dealing with perceptions ... The content of these perceptions is partly a contribution from a continuous physical object (unless the pain fades or the marble chips), partly a contribution from a continuous psychophysical subject .... The aesthetic work of art and object of criticism is not a continuant but an intermittent series of perceptions with a cumulative effect, namely, the perceptive series.

RC: All this is brought out in my book, <u>Mental Evolution and Art</u>, all the facts being discovered through phenomenological "scientific" tactics. This common end realization sort of supports the idea that there are "many ways to skin a cat," or to arrive at aesthetic processes at the highest level.

P: -we get the idea of a work of art being a multiple continuant on its physical side, we see that many kinds of works of art are so constituted. Prints, such as woodblocks, lithographs, etchings, have multiple continuants.

RC: Why not add Xerox copies?

P: -there are hundreds of copies of the book all of them equally good substitutes for one another.

RC: That is why I declared in writing that my book, <u>Mental Evolution and Art</u>, is a limited creative edition and as such, is aesthetic in itself, (I designed the jacket in order to have control and integration of the book's physical continuant - appearance) besides its aesthetic informative content.

P: Culture means a system of social relationships; and cultural objects are the instruments that mediate these relationships. ... Art is thus regarded as a cultural institution, and works of art as expressions of the culture of a period. Any single work of art is an item in this cultural expression... Wherever the perceptions of a work of art are directly <u>controlled</u> by tradition, there we have evidence of the action of a <u>cultural continuant</u>.

RC: Some of these "cultural continuants" are university art departments, commercial galleries, historical art museums, and traditionalist art columnists.

P: - the aesthetic work of art is not realized in any casual perception (as coming into the dental office with a fierce toothache or holding one's bladder in check) but is a <u>perceptive series</u> and involves <u>perceptual grasp</u> (overall realization).

RC: Pepper's "perceptual grasp" is analogous to my model's **"immediate aesthetic response."**

P: The aesthetic work of art actually involves a multiplicity of subjects, just as it involves a multiplicity of perceptions... Just as the aesthetic work of art is no single perception but the result of a total perceptive series, so the aesthetic work of art is not the perception of any one subject but a convergence effect among the perceptions of many subjects, which cancels out individual idiosyncrasies.

P: To summarize Pepper's view of the aesthetic, the following elements are identified:

A WORK OF ART INVOLVES:

1. A physical continuant

2. A subject continuant (the viewer)

3. A perceptive series with a funding effect (cumulative effect)

4. A perceptual grasp (overall reaction to the work)

5. A remote control over perception through:

6. A medium

7. Intrinsic ambiguities (for example, metaphoric elements)

8. Multiple physical continuants (whether many spectators coming up with a consensus of aesthetic quality of a work or situation)

9. "Unsensory perceptions" (perceptual control of other than sensory material; for example, the seepage of meanings and memories into the sensory aggregate that coagulates the whole into what is properly called a perception)

10. Cultural continuants

11. The subject continuant is always a multiple continuant

12. A convergence effect of every work of art through a. the constant physical continuant, b. the biological uniformity of the human subjects, c. a common culture, and d. the funding effect in the perceptive series - all of which tend towards a considerable objectivity and stability in the perceptive structure of the aesthetic

work of art.

... with due consideration of personal idiosyncrasies of inheritance, and the influences of environment and culture, there does not seem to be any insurmountable reason according to our analysis why highly objective judgments should not be obtainable not only of the aesthetic <u>content</u> of a work of art but also of its <u>aesthetic value</u>.

P: -Organicist: integrated perception

-Formist: normal perception

-Contextualist: vivid perception

-Mechanist: discriminating perception

-These perceptual demands emanate from the interpretations of aesthetic value intrinsic to the respective world hypotheses.

A COMPARISON WITH CHANG'S MODEL OF AESTHETIC PERCEPTION

My aesthetic model has been derived from over ten years of phenomenological searching for not just the real nature of art but also, as unconscious need for a <u>personalized and clarified philosophy</u>. One that integrates not only the divisions and compartments within the art world, but art with life itself. Thus I turned to personal experience and time to search for a unifying sense of all my socially separately learnings and activities. What does it all mean and what does it all add up for the meaning and quality of my life? Would each successive life situation and formal block of instruction in different fields add up to a rare realization that gains a purview of the contemporary reality (Great insight through <u>experienced perception</u>)? Could I gain a greater "perceptual grasp" than most by doing more than is normal?

So, like Pepper, I started adding up different viewpoints (of art instructors of what is good composition), and analyzing my successive experiences and perceptions in uncovering the processes of art, or more generally, the sense of beauty.

In mathematical form, the elements and their relationships are as such presented:

$$AA = r_o \left(\left[P + U + \frac{K_f}{K_d} + \frac{I_f}{I_d} \right]_o + r_a \left[\left(P + \frac{I_f}{I_d} + \frac{K_f}{K_d} \right) + G + M \right]_a \right) \Big/ (t + m)$$

Where,

AA = art appreciation
r_o = mental set or readiness of observer
r_a = mental set or readiness of artist
P = psychophysical stimuli and mental reactions
U = the Unconscious, including the irrational
K_f = knowledge of social origin that facilitates liking a specific something
K_d = knowledge of social origin that debilitates liking a specific something
I_f = Personal individual perceptual and Cognitive framework that facilitates liking something
I_d = Personal "preferences" that debilitate liking something
t = time
m = medium (−a) used
G = goal of the art work
M = material manipulation or transformation (technique)
o = observer's
a = artist's

Rodney Chang's model of art appreciation and perception, 1980 (guiding art philosophy for developing digital internet cyberart)

My model is based upon a quantitative sizing up of the potentially aesthetic material in order to come up with an integrated personal interpretation that supports a judgment of quality of experience and elicitation of the feeling of the aesthetic or art. Like a computer our brains sum up an aesthetic situation, subtracting the psychological turn-ons from the turn-offs, in order to almost simultaneously determine the resultant intensity of aesthetic quality felt from the stimulus. Much of the elements determining taste of course go on unconsciously and even automatically (one dogmatically rejects a certain brand of work or look). One "knows" what one likes and dislikes.

My model takes into consideration the actual effect that politics, capitalism and industrialization, social aesthetic conditioning, the unconscious and the personality of the spectator have on the final "grasp" of the aesthetic stimulus perceptually. The physical constituent (for example the canvas and paints themselves) of a work of art is thought of as just a stimulus for creative thinking that is passed from artist to spectator. When nobody looks or experiences in some other manner, there, strictly speaking, exists no "art" in the "work of art."

Quality is influenced by time and fashion. Popularity of materials (for example, digital tools for the 21st Century) to work with varies with the time and culture; goals for creating art change too. The aesthetic object or situation is the vehicle for active communication of feelings and awareness between two people, the artist and his public.

Norms come into play in the aesthetic experience by placing brakes on too sudden changes in art. It's like a stabilizing factor of the evolving art that is adapting to our new needs. Thus does my model incorporate formistic thought. Just as my approach to isolating the spontaneous aesthetic perception (which leads to appreciation) is one of cumulating and summation, so is its nature quite mechanistic as a view of human nature. Psychophysical elements are definitely included, for the physiological sensations of art media play excitatory and therefore sensuous roles for the aesthetic experience. The model is "hedonistic" in that it defines everything that adds up (or subtracts from) to an aesthetic experience as "art appreciation" or pleasurable.

Of course the model is highly organistic in nature, for it states that larger entities, like art appreciation or aesthetic experience, are the accumulation of other multi-level relationships of the human mind. The model points to the possibility of creating new art with universal appeal; it serves as a tool to create art defended by art criticism standards of the different world hypotheses. For example, Da Waiting Room is the aesthetic manifestation of 1) an individual's attempt to make his environment and psychological space integrated and thus reflect his personality to others, 2) the realization that the aesthetic experience can be found in real life situations besides traditional objects of art (contextualistic), and 3) everything in the world, including seemingly conflicting goals and situations, can be interrelated at a higher level of unified harmony, once creative insight and problems are worked out to mold the final aesthetic refinement of a work of art. The cited artwork challenges the norm of contemporary art, not to dethrone art but to serve as catalyst for further growth and direction (real life situations) of this new form of art.

From such an eclectic (just like my "personality") model of aesthetic perception can be drawn a personal philosophy, an accidental reward for the continued and disciplined study of art. I call it **Transformative Philosophy**. That's a fancy term that stands for a view of the world as one characterized by constant evolution through adaptive and maladaptive change, which at the same time, maintains a constant relativity of all phenomena and things. Reality is relative, and so are facts. Evidence cannot pinpoint an ultimate reality but only support present or emerging hypotheses of these changing relationships of specific things tied to a higher order of permanent unity. The wholeness of the universe is expressed as the final answer to personal conflict and aesthetic value. It is my duty to discern how all these different fields of study have interconnections that can be expressed aesthetically as a method of proving their existence. My art shall be based upon attention to change (in the world and in art) attached to a higher level of organization that maintains a sense of universal (or natural) unity among the artist, the spectators and work of art. **(This was written prior to the computer, its derivative digital art, and the virtual world of the Internet and its global cyberculture becoming a part of the artist's life)**

Note: (2001)-*My art shall be based upon attention to change (in the world* - high technology-*and in art*-digital art) *attached to a higher level of organization* (the internet) *that maintains a sense of universal (or natural) unity among the artist* (integration with art history, traditional media and digital expression), *the spectators* (global virtual community) *and work of art* (online cyberart).

Rodney E. J. Chang

The Chaotic Existence of the Computer Artist

- a theory of integration among Darwinism, chaos theory, art psychological processes, computer graphic systems, and oil painting April 5, 1996 by Pygoya a.k.a. Rodney Chang, A.A.,B.A.,B.A.,M.A.,M.A., M.A.,M.A.,MS.Ed.,D.D.S.,Ph.D. (at the time of this writing not yet on the Internet) Figures for this chapter are located in Appendix 2 pg.154

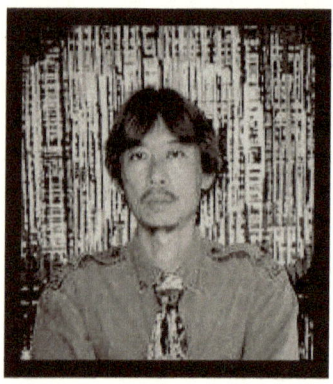

Pygoya 1997

In 1997 Pygoya established Lastplace.com and
began referring to himself first as a "cyberartist" (1997)
then as a "Webist" (2003)

(HISTORICAL NOTE- this article includes first thoughts that led to the written Manifesto of Webism launched online in 2003- see bold type paragraph)

Computer graphic programs and its finite deterministic "canned" (preprogrammed effects not made by the artist using the software) are "organisms" in the context of nonlinear dynamical systems ecology that compete with the rest of the pool of commands for space (computer memory) and time (in central processing unit; CPU) for survival in the making of computer or digital art. Time for the command has limiting factors such as the hardware's speed of computing which is inversely proportionately related to the artist's/user's waiting time (down time creatively unless the brain is pondering the next move or doing other system chores) *during* processing manipulation of the command. There's a (yawn) wait or busy signal on the screen. So making art with the computer is process more than results like any other complex dynamical nonlinear system of world events as described by chaos and fractal theories. Making computer art is best facilitated when the artist is positioned mentally on the *edge of chaos*, waiting for accentuated visual breakthroughs when unpredicted, sudden changes occur in the *phase transition* domain of the statistical chaos world and model. Not all (computer) artists work alike. Not all artists do what they do for the sake of (making) art. Not all artists know what and why they work. Enter psychotherapist importance in the well being of the stand-alone working artist, especially when the financial rewards for long-term commitment isn't there. But for this particular artist, myself as a case study, phenomenological as artist-researcher I have a clear picture of what my life as an artist over thirty years has been about - as diagnosed by my new acquaintance of fractal and chaos theory, new concepts of reality taking root in the 80's and endangering science as it has been practiced prior to these mathematical model discoveries.

Like any other artist young and raw but with latent talent, I sought to improve and develop through formal schooling and dedicated work, work, and work in the "studio" until the work got better - more polished. I could tell way back that my work "sucked" but it did not stop me from believing it would get better - far better than the average artist's output. Because in my mind the ideal images laden with fresh artistic ideas were visible. But limited technical skills hampered its real world manifestation for others to see and appreciate. Enter the computer, personal and affordable in the mid-eighties. At first it was a new toy with all these magical effects, including making routine blends of colors automatically that only a master watercolorist could do previously. Technical ability all of a sudden wasn't a premium to being a good artist, just its recognition of quality and incorporation into one's ideas for creating art. My art's visual details suddenly got much better but to me it was normal baseline stuff for any professional artist, nothing new in itself. For ten years now, new art could come from some other source besides professional level traditional art media techniques, now available to anybody who bothers to "read the manual".

Up to prior to reading up on "chaos" I saw myself as some sort of solitary saboteur of the traditions of art and its establishments with all their ingrained biases and defensiveness against the new, like any other field. There are, even in art, powers that be, that do not want to be overthrown by obsolescence and irrelevance to the changing times. I thought of myself as relatively passive but mere operator or catalyst to the ever-growing power of graphic software. I, in a certain way, was playing a game as artist, attempting to get the freshest imagery from the latest version of software with the minimum of time and effort. I can be selfish, on the edge of laziness as an artist. I figure with so much artistic firepower with computers as my art "medium", I shouldn't have to work as long and as hard as traditional artists to produce significant bodies of work. And just to rebel from the platform of defensiveness maintained by almost all other computer artists (actually I have never heard any other artist take my position), I claim the computer itself to be AN ARTIST, not a "dumb tool" with the user-artist in control as the creator. I stated that the stuff I have displayed in hundreds of exhibits, including museums, has been collaboration between at least two players, the user and the machine. But in fact I considered myself the lesser in importance, intentionally taking a back seat as observer of the progress and graduated increases in power of both graphic software and the operating hardware capacity over time. I merely "drove" these machines with software as the latest octane to see how fast, how far they could take me on my journey to becoming a better (and better) artist. Once I was satisfied with my current work then I feared I would stop making art, stop being an artist. Several times I thought I had come close to that treacherous place in the artist's life. But I always came back to the well and commenced making new efforts to go further. Maybe because I couldn't help notice new graphic software, new games in all these mail order product magazines that junk up my business mail as a dentist in private practice (my "real job" and patron role in support of the "starving artist"). I looked forward when my job would be complete, fostering the inclusion of artificial intelligence into the scheme of things for the working digital artist. To this day what I have to work with seems really primitive, almost stupid.

We WILL be light years ahead in decades to come in regards to what we have to work with as user-artists on personal computers. That's why I delight to be deliberate in bothering to work in the NOW (and the past 10 years during the BEGINNING of PC art making ability) producing paintings on canvas - for posterity. Yes it "documents" my artistic life on the computer as artist but it also importantly documents the evolution of computer graphic power for personal computers. The 1980s paintings I live with now on my walls to me have a sense of "antiquity". Although they look "futuristic" to the naive viewer of art, they look primitive to me and probably to the knowledgeable programmer who would see the vintage graphic giveaway marks of the derived imagery. Collaborating with artisans (artist in their own right) to execute the paintings from my computer generated image "blueprints" was/is part of my position that I am just a cog in the overall process of making new art with the computer. The computer, the software programmer (even if the product is intended to make profits by assisting commercial graphic types make their ads and not for inspired use by serious artists to help embody their noble ends), the painter and the computer user/artist all are part of the team that manufactures the new art for the new world known as the Global Village in our new Information Age.

So much for my background as a working artist using the computer. A formal background in science (dentistry, zoology), art (MA, MA, AA) and art psychology (Ph.D.) has served me well to have a makeshift model-theory by which to work with purpose and an art philosophy (scroll to bottom portion) by which to live and with a sense of meaning and purpose for existing. Cut to the present, to my new promised enlightenment through exposure of chaos and complexity theories.

The analogy drawn here is between Darwin's ideas of natural selection of species in a limiting environment and statistical models describing chaotic behavior in real world complex dynamical nonlinear systems, such as a unique snowflake forming in the atmosphere with eventual falling to the ground. In my situation, as I am starting to see things, I (I emphasize the "I") AM the ENVIRONMENT, the ecology. Graphic programs are populations of species called COMMANDS. With programs at my perusal I potentially have unlimited visual effects that I could conjure up as a computing artist. Limitations to this infinite graphic power manifestation include current level of graphic effects programmed (state of the art graphic programming, itself limited by hardware capability), economics of making the art, making the electronic products for today's consumer market and amount of time vested into working in my electronic "studio" as a "part-time" artist with a "regular (self supporting) job". As it turns out in my case the TIME in the studio per session hovers around a CONSTANT. I probably average 1-2 hours of "access" time to making art before life's demands curtail extended further working time (such as family scheduled routines, going to sleep to have sufficient rest for the next work day). Since I am goal oriented and aim for one or more completed works of art per session, I unconsciously have built up an efficient methodology even as it pertains to deriving everlasting works of art. In other words, I have "x" amount of time to OUT PUT and get these pixels moving into rightful positions on the screen to elicit in myself, ultimately the cruelest of art critics, satisfactory material that I call confidently not just "art" but "new art". So within the limiting parameters of TIME I unconsciously have to be SELECTIVE in which commands of the array available in many different programs available as my computer "system". They COMPETE with each other as they COHABITATE in my internal hard drive for selective USE, for processing time when active RAM give them visual life on screen, as each command contributes to the final image saved as a work of art. So how do I choose what to use, in limited time to get immediate results (granted other computer artists don't work in this impatient, instant gratification style but can spend months on perfecting a single image - we're all different, especially as artist)? Turns out, adopting the chaos theory to form analogous links to my complex and dynamic PROCESS (as any artistic endeavor is to other creators of artwork), I AM the ecology in which commands live, interact, adapt, compete, survive, multiply or become extinct! It all happens unconsciously in my mind, through my work habits according to chaos theory!

Specifically, through the user's personalized sense of values, efficiency and productivity to create (the goal) change (new art), software is manipulated via image processing in search of "mutations" of visual effects, different but probably evolved from what already had previously been visualized, experienced, and accomplished by the artist. My life work "develops" as my body of work, using a multitude of different computer platforms (hardware) and software, "evolves" over time. Only the most "successful" software commands are routinely used in processing while others fall into disuse, becoming "extinct" in my active computer graphic visual vocabulary. These cannot compete with newer effects which may be more complex visually (thereby more interesting to the artist), become trite or boring over time (thereby repetitious, such as "fad" graphics like color gradients in my earlier work) or be consumed by new software commands that include the old effect in a composite more complex visual effect. In fact with the accumulation of bench time at the computer I have unconsciously developed habitual use of sequences of graphic commands, predictable in overall effects which at this point I consider PLEASING and thus contributory and INDIGENOUS to my signature artist STYLE. These clusters of commands have withstood the test of time and continue to survive as part of my active ecology of commands by which I make my next work of art. Such whirls of commands co-adapted not only to my way of working but symbiotic to each other (I need to use together to get certain effects) can be considered certain "traits" that have evolved not unlike "attractors" identified in dynamical nonlinear systems. My artwork falls into these twirls of modes of creating graphic marks, then haphazardly move on to other clusters of commands for further processing toward some ultimate pictorial end. Over time, groups of such graphic attractors accumulate as part of the artist's working method, thereby producing a sort of CONSTANCY and STABILITY of the completed results. The different pieces all look like they were done by the same artist (even if different programs were used and such programs were not made by the artist). A recognizable artistic "style" is born. But as the same attractors are used a sense of rut, of stagnancy eventually arrives. All the new works begin to become simple refinements of previous works. Of course galleries like to see that. New works are identifiable by even the naive collector as the latest work of artwork of an artist whose earlier work has already appreciated in financial value. But to not change, like a natural ecosystem, would be the kiss of death, of extinction of the artist's endeavors. Luckily, in the computer artist's sphere of activity, temptation as a kick in the butt, to take on risk for change, arrives in the offering of new graphic power embodied in available new software. With a sudden jolt of a new effect from a new program added into the internal drive's command POPULA-TION, such a small change of visual effect can cause an avalanche of change in the total image. The operator's fascination with this new, seductive command/product challenges all previous adapted commands that constitute his previous work for time and reten-tion in the studio. If artistic studio time remains constant then that means some older commands will be eliminated in order to complete a work of art at the end of each time limited session. Survival of the fittest. Sudden potential new change to the final product's look - new software potentiates the possibility of taking the artist and computer into the realm of "phase transition" or the "edge of chaos" where creativity is maximally potentiated and most efficient.

"Co-evolution" occurs when the artist works simultaneously with several programs. On a more "global" scale, programs with all its species of commands become extinct when they fall into disuse (obsolescence). But other programs link together to create effects as genetic components of the established artistic style. As the art-ist's selection changes the pool of hybrid art genes (commands) adapts in this new design and pattern ecology, displaying the latest development of artistic style. With new effects from newly intro-duced programs radical change can occur to the "morphology" of the artwork's appearance.

As processing units become faster with more megahertz bang-for-the-buck, I as artist can incorporate more commands into RAM action for the same amount of working time that's con-figured to my schedule and temperament. The more commands used the more "complexity" of design, of pattern, of artistic state-ment. In nonlinear complex dynamical systems a simple and small change can create sweeping change. As such a small new com-mand sequence can inspire a very transformed "mutated" image. Being parsimonious with my time as artist, the greed to discover/experience new effects (new art) is counterbalanced by the risk of unpredictable lost of time and effort. There have been many loss sessions when I used new software to create with and ended up only with garbage. More megahertz also enables me to be more liberal with the range of commands to be used in a session. Some not so dramatic effects are included as a refining ingredient that supports the more visually aggressive commands' effects that jump out at the viewer. With such expansion of the number and the range of effects, the cumulative image pattern is MORE COM-PLEX. The more complex, the more chance of random and chaotic consequences. Another influence on the art making ecology with the ability of faster change is visual UNIFORMITY. Consistent use of attractors (clusters of command sequences) can be done quicker, serve as the basic baseline/foundation of one's habitual style from which new commands for new effects can be planted in, merged and experimented with the established, all within the allotted working period. As such, with increased processing time, the environment or "climate" for making computer art stabilizes as all these idiosyncratic "whirls" of attractor clusters of commands become constants, predictable in the works of art.

As the computer art body of works grows and evolves eventually a niche will be established in the art world. Currently much resistance to such hybrid man-machine made art exists. Traditional galleries, museums, artists, collectors, critics, and historians become fearful. Done by hand with excruciating patience with the prerequisite endurance of repetitious detailing still sells. Pain and suffering by artist is still equated with good work. The results of such skilled labor then are snatched up by rich collectors. But technology spawns its own culture. Look at the techie, geeky language now emerging on the Internet. **Eventually those that live in that Global Village through specific artistic cyber-sites will crave for more. For pictures that not just mirror past world experience in online cyberspace or virtual reality, but for art created and born from the womb of technology herself. By bypassing regionalism, permitting the young East and West to talk, interact with each other, immediacy of global review instead of post-dated unreal time restraint, there is the promise of the propagation of a digital art appreciation (leading to eventual sales) outside of the present mainstream art world. We could possibly create a new art form that emerges from within global cyberspace, in order to fulfill the basic human need of having culture (*cyberculture*) wherever we roam. On the Internet the art of the real art world become merely REPRODUCTIONS**

in the virtual world, becoming less COMPETITIVE with the electronic first generation art imagery in this new art market niche. It's not too far fetch to consider the extinction of art and its marketplace, as we now know it, after the development and proliferation of the Global Village in the next few centuries. Electronic art would go hand in hand with digital money, transactions, telecommunications, in a mature real time global society. With the further development of interactive art making, self-reproducing graphic programs incorporating artificial intelligence, the art evolves, entrenches in its niche, dominates the art ecology and enhances the democratization of art making for all.

In summary I, as computer artist, now see differently in adopting the chaos and complexity model as my modus operandi for making art. I continue to use canned software, geared to commercial art application, in a way that challenges the deterministic visual effects guaranteed effortlessly by faithfully using the manual like a cookbook. My personal style evolves along with new commands thrown into the environment that I choose to work in, including its restraints of time, effort, technical proficiency and monetary funds. To accomplish new personified art I mix software effects, interbreed command effects, let attractors clusters adapt and compete for survival use, repetitively do the same procedures that evoke a common style but at the same time seek to live at the edge of chaos by seeking instability, revolutionary turmoil to my style through rebelliously throwing new commands as they become available into the stew.

When I first approached reading about fractals and chaos theory I thought it may open my eyes to something going on IN the computer as I used computer programs to make art. After all I knew scientists had succeeded in simulating "artificial life" in programming. For example one program creates numerical species that reproduce, compete, adapt and become extinct in their simulated ecosystem. One other program creates mutants of biomorphic patterns that evolve in the program but require input by the operator to instruct modifying or guided influences on the actual mutations. Here we have an interactive mutating system between computer and user. But in my case the current graphic programs are "dumb" from a self-evolving point of view.

I, the operator-artist, initiate any "change" in my line of completed artworks, which in turn really reflects the change in the active fauna of commands in my repertoire to make digital art at that point in time. The programs themselves are actually LINEAR in function. That is, activate one direction of the program via a command and one corresponding effect occurs in the image on the screen. It's one to one correspondence, change in x results in a direct proportionate change in y. On a graph using x and y as coordinates a straight line is produced. Nonlinear, non-dynamic, simple reaction between two factors. But in a nonlinear, complex dynamic system of a probable fundamental and universal process in all complex systems, the relationship between x and y is more muddled. A graph in such a system produces a slight convex curve - other influences unknown or unforeseen confound the interaction dissected out by man between x and y. So, in my art process case, my work over time does not get proportionately better in a linear way. Changes in the nature of the works are based not on natural selection processes as in the above stated experimental programming for change/mutation but on AESTHETIC SELECTION BY THE OPERATOR. To my surprise, chaos theory seems to be operational in my art process as a computer artist but the dynamics going on is OUTSIDE the computer, INSIDE my head, in my behavior patterns. For this behavior to change there is either changes in the character of the commands (new programs, rediscovery of unused commands by rereading the manual) OR major changes in my life or lifestyle. For example what if suddenly I was retired as a dentist? It increases the odds that my constant time that I now plug into the electronic art studio might change. I'll have more "free time" to sustain longer lasting graphic explorations in the speculation for new art.

During the Cambrian period of our earth there was a boom in major new morphological forms in the fossil records never seen before or after again. Theorists think some sort of mass extinction opened up unfulfilled biological niches and there was a mad biological rush to claim niche stakes. Nature was meta-creative! Forms are estimated to evolve at the phyla level - major different types of creatures. Thereafter evolutionary changes, mutations were not as drastic but more of improving, modifying, and refining form for better fitness in the inhabited niches. An analogy is drawn to my output of computer art dated back since 1985. On my first venture into the digital graphic world my artistic life changed. With all the possibilities of graphic marks to be discovered I felt like a kid in the candy shop for the first time. I buzzed from command by command, testing effects and composing adequate early works with everything I could get my hands on. In a sense I was like a cat, leaving my scent, my mark, everywhere claiming my territory, my visual turf with the newly available graphic software power yet not popular with the masses of traditional artist still residing in their own world. My book, Rodney Chang:Computer Artist (1990, Creative Frontiers, HI), should have been titled, Rodney Chang:Computer Artist, Cambrian Period. It's hard, after reviewing all the images (100) in the book to link them all to the same artist through one identifiable style. But at the time that was the goal, to demonstrate the versatility of the new art medium with all its novel visual effects unseen up to then (in my opinion) in the history of other art media. Like newly developing living organism in a new self-supporting broth, my art productivity teemed with sudden and exciting new shapes and forms. This new found sphere of working as an artist is characterized by the largest collection of graphic commands that I have used at one time to make computer art. My entry into computer graphics bordered on the fanatic. I found myself working with six different computers, going broke attempting to keep up with all the different software for each hardware system and its constantly update versions. Fill out all those software ownership registration cards (proof of purchase) and mail them out! The rationale back then was to produce imagery that could be characteristic of the hardware (and complementing software) for each brand of personal computer, such as the Amiga, Atari, Mac, Tandy and IBM machines. Today it seems my art output over ten years conforms to a sort of power law distribution in the number of commands regularly used in making art in a specific session. A power law distribution of x and y is not linear but forms a slight convex curve. If one studies my output over the years, especially my Paintouts series (computer images rendered as oil on canvases, now numbering about 180), change/mutation of the image may be related to change quantitative (set of commands used) besides qualitative (improvement or new graphic commands over the years). If the stuff used to make the pictures, commands as building blocks for the art change, then the resultant picture transforms. The artwork is the residue of the dynamic process of commands aesthetically selected by the operating artist with behaviors true to some underlying fundamental universal process, complex, dynamical and somewhat unpredictable.

It is merely weeks since I have become acquainted with chaos theory and the possibility that I AM an artist working chaotically. What happens now should I permanently adopt this belief system in my future work? There's a chance, after identifying specific important players in my process, that I may pay special attention to such elements in the production of my work. For example I may now attempt to consciously manipulate the number of commands I use per session or intentionally eliminate some of my most adapted, favorably entrenched commands to see how the imagery changes. Forced extinction or conscious manipulation to attempt to avoid stabilized ruts and get back to the "edge" of chaos to rediscover artistic defeat and inventivity at an accelerated rate. I could see my past (and future) works in a new light - actually do a controlled study of chaotic statistics to quantify chaotic functional relationships among the 180 digital canvas works completed. My body of works may serve yet another application - a test of chaos and complexity mathematical theory that holds up and applies, this time in the complex process of making art. And although I describe all this phenomena merely as a digital artist, could these underlining universal processes have been going on PRIOR to my computerized artistic life? What is the meaning of my having earned ten college degrees? Could it have been that the times were ripe (my college years, 60s-90s) to rebel from the fragmented "fields" of knowledge, endlessly extending such bodies by adding on bits and pieces to each respective isolated field, totally disconnected to other fields, to the "big picture"? This was the start up time (late 60s, early 70s) of the "multidisciplinary" approach to education in the "university without walls", the start up in certain mathematicians' and physicists' heads on the concepts of chaos as something different from the classic Scientific Method upon which all modern research and the building up of these separate fields of knowledge are founded. I intuitively was looking for answers BETWEEN the bodies of knowledge I was fed - art, psychology, dentistry, teaching, counseling, biology, communications, among others. What were the LINKS, commonalties among analogous concepts in different fields? How could I describe them, being aware of these links ahead of my educational cultural format, as an artist? What led me to make relevant, significant art down the road of life? Why try to do everything as an artist - painting, sculpture, photography, ceramics, mixed media, installations? Was I that good (like Picasso?) or was I just doing internships with each courted media, unconsciously searching for a common underlying universal force in the artistic process? Why study something I labeled "Art Psychology" when dabbling with psychological theories was taboo for the art graduate student? Why write a book on the mental evolution of man as described in my books as "mental ontogeny recapitulates mental phylogeny"? Why label it "Transformative Psychology" and take on this view, this belief, of psychology as process for myself as a working artist? Could it have been, without realizing it, that I was setting myself up to be the ultimate chaotic artist? A discotheque in the dental office (1979)? Insane? Or yet another fearless decision to stir up my life with unexpectancies, nonconformity, uncharacteristic problems and challenges, in other words, relatively more chaos than other dentists have to deal with in their daily experience of professional life. So even as a dentist outside the art studio was I attempting to be true to setting up my life situation to learn from personal phenomenological experience, conflict and adaptation-even during my clinical hours? Did I already place myself in an environmental art test tube, for unpredictable results that could influence my ongoing artistic growth process? I continue to ask these nagging questions of myself over the years. Now I have a theory as working model to help make sense out of all this previous self inflicted situations and reactive behavior. And if all this underlying chaos processing was already in motion BEFORE I turned into a Benedict Arnold "computer artist" (not considered a "real artist" in Hawaii in the 80s), what inference can we make about other traditional artists? Are there in fact statistical distribution of behavior formulas governing their own artistic process (besides the so-called tapping into the universal creative spirit like some claim) that, unknown to them, are "pulling their strings", and as such enslaving them to impulsively sustain personal identities as artist, resulting in creative works, even if there is minimal economic compensation for such productivity?

A positive self-realization is the result of familiarity with my new readings in chaos as artist. Before I was merely a "catalyst", the necessary crank to initiate self-perpetuating visual results. I would wait for programmers to make progress (new "versions") for my own work to advance. I was in a supportive role, complacent to wait for artificial intelligence to enter graphic programming so computer art would really hit the fan as an art form. Suddenly my perspective has changed. THE COMPUTER, THE SOFT-WARE, THE SPECIFIC COMMANDS OF PROGRAMS ARE NOT IMPORTANT. It's ME by whom the art is created by using programs with all its building blocks, its strands of 0s and 1s that comprise processing instructions, that add up to more than the sum of all those commands. Hey, it's (using the computer as medium) a MANUAL thing (not the underlying universal process that describes my art process)! I don't have to blame my art's shortcomings on the limits of today's computer technology. Newer, super graphic effects is supplemental "gravy", actually catalysts that potentially shake up my armamentarium of digital art making tools. Yes, my work does transcend the deterministic nature of programmers' offerings. My computer art mirrors MY SENSITIVITY, MY VITALITY, MY EXPRESSION as aesthetic selection among the potential pool of graphic tools (commands), retiring some, adapting to new forms, as I continue my journey, my quests, living the artistic life - chaotically.

Early computer graphic programs were cruder and inflexible in enabling the user to customize marks. It gave the operator the fundamental graphic effects of color gradients blended like a professional, geometric uniformly "fills" of any color, basic popular "brush" marks with unadjustable width, saturation and uniformity of color, spotty airbrushing simulation, etc. It was more difficult to hide, as artist claiming authorship of the computer image, the program with which the work was executed on the monitor. Today more program complexity is available through more available memory per effect and quicker processing rates (megahertz's) for programmers to work with in producing practical software for commercial artists and amateurs dabbling in computer graphics. I judge authorship from the amount of distancing from manual directed results in the image. If one takes a section on the image, can others recognize individuality or is it all canned visual effects of the software? With certain programs there are now parameters by which one can "customize" one's graphic marks, such as the size, brushstroke character and density of the mark relative to the pressure of the input device and its speed of execution. But to me the ultimate criterion for originality that severs the control of the software is the global IDEA of the image more so than its graphic constituents. It's not how fancy the fonts are but what a poem says, to draw an analogy. To insure total oblivion of the detailed minutia of a pixel-based mark and its dispersal from software commands, I have the captured computer image painted by hand. This "post-production" after digital discovery tends to eliminate any pixel level detail as trivial. In a sense visual scaling effects of the pixel level visible at my relatively low-resolution level of working (600x400 resolution) is eliminated through painting on canvas with a real brush. Of course all the traditional values of responding (conditioned respect for paintings) to an "original oil on canvas" come into play in the appreciation of the aesthetic image. But the most exciting thing now is that the output from computer graphic imagery is now NOT computer based but just another painting. To further downplay my rejection on the worshipping of tedious and detailed craftsmanship as the mainstay of authorship I commission out the execution of the painting to another painter, using my computer printout and slide as "blueprints".

Hopefully the resulting painting impacts the viewer through the composing of IDEAS and FEELINGS with graphic constituents merely the substrate to support the latter. Such ideas and feelings surface from the deep well of the right hemisphere of our brain. When totally absorbed in the creative process, the artist draws from a multitude of levels of consciousness, many of which he or she is totally unaware of. Execution of such subjective resources of the artistic mind then foster works of art through the filtering methodology of chaos theory as applicable to creative art production.

Acquaintance with the possible influence of chaos phenomena on my art process and work has been therapeutic. The specific visual effects of the multitude of software, past, present, and future are not as important to the appearance of my work. It is I, the operator, that dictates the limits with which the computer assists in the making of art. With the multitude of time consuming choices via commands I must select what to use, in what order, and for what means. Since I am an abstractionist that does not start with preconceived subject matter, my process is more governed by losing myself in the flow of the process that reveals itself progressively on the digital screen. No resistance is put up to halt the subconscious in becoming involved with intuitive, driven (and sidetracked) directives. Although the process is guided by formal aesthetic values rooted in my formal art education and polished by 30 years of art making, effort is made to buffer what occurs to happen without censorship. Chaos theory also sheds new light upon interconnections among different academic disciplines such as those fenced from one another in the artist's experience of higher education. I now see that although specific results supporting fact of different experiments describe different phenomena of our world, all follow some sort of underlying rhythm of behavior in an orderly regularity in a SEEMINGLY chaotic natural universe. This basic truth is a part of our art through history.

Figures appear in Appendix 2 on page 154.
Figure 1 - Power law distribution characteristic of statistical complex dynamical systems
Figure 2 - Pygoya's theory of the order and formulation of art

References-
Chaos, James Gleick, 1987
Complexity, Life at the Edge of Chaos, Roger Lewin, 1992
Mental Evolution and Art, Rodney Chang, 1980
Rodney Chang:Computer Artist, Rodney Chang, 1990

Rodney E. J. Chang

The Psychology of Art and Digital Art

Pygoya (Rodney Chang)
November 15, 1999

As a graduate student in aesthetics I concluded art is *psychological* at its core. Fun explorations included imaginary interviews with famous deceased 20th century artists such as Picasso, Kandinsky and Matisse. This entailed reviewing their autobiographic writings and published dialogue with interviewers during their lifetime. Besides this approach in my quest to answer for myself, just "What IS art?" I reviewed psychological models and theories of the human psyche. From such an idiosyncratic approach to the study of art I reaped a personal insight into what I wanted to accomplish, to *be*, as an artist - for life. This was 1980. Thereafter I held faith in an art philosophy to guide my creative efforts to fulfill my potential talent. For the scientist in me I selected the phenomenological experimental approach to invent new art. Such an operational platform freed me to start anew, disregard the past, and exploit any means by which to create new vision.

Finding the time to pursue a personal answer to "what is art," a luxury of time while also confronting the demands of life, was five years before my introduction to the personal computer as a promising art tool. During this interval between theory and practice (1980-84) I courted traditional art media in search of a commitment to a specific art medium. I believe my style of visual expression is embedded in all of my digital art, the same that developed during these formative years of dabbling in painting, printmaking, photography, ceramics and mixed media. In 1984 I had finally "committed" to bronze sculpture, only to have my interest completely divorced with a serendipitous introduction to computer graphics. Thereafter it really never mattered to me that it was "digital" rather than some other, more socially acceptable, art medium. I had long before started a quest to develop as a professional artist, producing work worthy of public recognition due to its honest manifestation of my unique feelings and personality.

My initial approach to creating with a computer was to start with a blank screen, to me a *tabula rasa*. I remember staring into the mysterious blank screen of pitch black. It was the exciting discovery of a three-dimensional space, not phosphorous ignited on a surface but to me uncharted virgin territory in the fine arts. I felt like a pioneer with the golden opportunity to stake out aesthetic turf, years prior to the arrival of the Internet's WWW. Some maintained the commercial graphics tradition of starting a project with a scan of physical world reality captured through photography, then do graphic editing work to make an altered statement. Conversely I was intrigued by the novel mere building block for making art, the solitary pixel. This visual element, like a particle shot from an airbrush, was paired with my ready-made philosophical and psychological models from *Transformative Psychology*, a part of my adopted *Art Psychology*.

Most artists depart to explore their talent from the safe and proven harbor of art history. New works can thus be explained and accepted as part of an established tradition of aesthetic worth. Knowing and using such an accepted visual "language" make new works extensions of the historical precedents, progressing art in a natural continuum from an approved starting point.

I instead choose to jump off the edge of familiarity, create without history clouding my creative intuition, start with a tool which had no mark in art history. Instead of history I selected psychology to navigate my journey through the maze of time and self-discovery to formulate a creditable new fine art. Art not just "new" because it had a totally different appearance (stereotypical early computer graphics) but because of the guidance of a new psychology as the alchemy for an eccentric mind.

I, as artist, of course harbored no prejudice against the computer, although in the beginning I must confess paranoia of the computer someday replacing me, and even possibly destroying my developed artistic sensitivity from previous work in painting and sculpture. But after all this risk taking I stand at the eve of 2000 as a survivor of the process, with the realization that I have been fortunate, that such a maverick approach for an artist searching for inspiration has been heuristic, not detrimental, to my achieved current results. The work I exhibit in the 1999 India exhibition is the harvest from seeds of thought and action planted as far back as

1975 when I was a graduate student in both art and psychology, as well as persistent effort in the *cyber-studio*.

Just what is the psychology that contributes to the appearance and content of my digital Web-based art?

The theories of Transformative Psychology are published in my book, <u>Mental Evolution and Art</u> (Exposition Press, New York, New Work, 1980). The main tenet is that "mental ontogeny recapitulates mental phylogeny." Or more simply stated, as living organisms duplicate past primordial forms of life during its embryonic stages *in urtero*, the morphological structure may be paired with yet undiscovered   neurological function compatible to support the physical form observed. In other words, could not the embryonic fetus that, during the period looks like a fish (gills and tail apparent), also process environmental information *like* a fish? From this radical thought (would be interesting to conduct neurological research that did comparative brain activity studies for different species during the same embryonic fetal facsimiles) came the idea of the existence of infinite levels of consciousness within the human brain, many of which remain latent and unexplored, remnants of our long lost ancestral past. For example, the levels we identify as the "subconscious" (Freud), the unconscious, the hypnotic state, day dreaming, dreaming, hallucination, mental telepathy and the different levels of sleep as depicted by brain wave recordings. I hypothesized that such a "human nature" affect the way people "see" and "feel" what we call art. Such a theory would explain submerged past experience as the source for statements at art shows like "I don't understand art but I know what I like" or the artist just knowing that "it works" and therefore when a work is complete. Or the instincts of early elementary school children to place figures of animals or humans on the bottom border of a drawing on paper, no matter what culture the children reside in. Or conflicting preferences by the same individual in judging art when in the hypnotic state as opposed to choices made during the usual conscious state. Or the natural affinity of children towards bright primary colors versus the more subdued tertiary colors which we later find in more "sophisticated", "mature" works of art.

Using such a psychology as my launching pad, I attempt to create on the computer without specific subject matter in mind.

Somewhat akin to automatic doodling and letting loose feelings similar to the Abstract Expressionists, I hope to capture imagery that triggers not only my deeper levels of consciousness but also strike similar chords within the audience, no matter how illiterate they are in the canons of art history. I desire to create art that takes the viewer to the most common denominator of aesthetic response; the awakening of deep seeded feelings he or she never knew existed. Do that and there is a natural attraction to my imagery, worthy of holding the viewer's attention. Through such a strategic approach do I hope to bring forth for all a common reaction that only fine art can precipitate. By such artistic intent the ground is somewhat leveled for both the uneducated with no formal art education and scholar of aesthetics. A universal response is summoned that suggests we are all the same.

In conclusion, realize that I consider the adaptation of my creative efforts to the medium of computers as secondary in the judgment of my output of art's worthiness as significant contribution to culture.

Beyond Computer Art

November 18, 1999

My concern about the nature of art is the primary anteced-
ent to my use of computers to produce fine arts imagery. For over
thirty years (1970-2000) what I made paralleled my theoretical
concerns about art. Such concerns are rooted in my time and culture as a working artist. But besides the absorption and reflecting back of popular Western culture and its aesthetic expressions,
was a burning desire to make art that was meaningful to myself.
I needed a deep conviction to stay involved in art for life, not superficially produce pleasant things to pass the time away. It needed
to be cerebral.

In art school I accepted the notion that the work of art is an
object in itself, not some illusory visual trick to serve as a window
of escape from one's confining physical reality. The painting was
an animate thing that existed in its own right. The back, the sides
wrapping around the supporting stretchers were as real an entity as
the painted surface. I adopted the ideas of Ad Reinhardt, Donald
Judd and the Minimalists. For such a restricted approach to art,
formalistic visual attributes and control provide the embodiment
of the idealized object. Only attention to meticulous detail could
eventually lead to the perfect brushstroke, the intricately balanced,
complex, abstract composition. I needed to develop a "sensitivity"
to my art materials, feel the plastic quality of paint, and viscerally
appreciate a freely applied, developed control through practice,
graphite mark on fibrous paper. Art school taught me the sensual-
ity of aesthetic surfaces and forms.

After a decade of this attention to detail, craft took a back
seat to my burning desire to gain a more profound insight into
the nature of the aesthetic. I wanted to go beyond my contemporaries' preoccupation with the art making issues of the day. I
searched beyond the confines of art history. The answers for me
came from the discipline of psychology that in turn led to adop-
tion of an alternative reason for being an artist. Through the study
of the human psyche art became more than just an isolated object

existing within its own contrived reality. I became aware of the art object as a strong stimulus that generated an aesthetic response. I had made a 180 degree shift from bringing objects into existence to constructing environments endowed with aesthetic stimuli to produce shared multimedia experience. For example, I became my own imaginary model for future figure sculpture as I discoed on the dance floor in my dental clinic reception area.

From here it was easy to encompass any physical material to create art as an enriched part of life. Materiality was just one element in creating the stimulus for predictable aesthetic response from a targeted audience. Such was my frame of mind when I stumbled fortuitously on the personal computer. I recognized from the start that within this black box resided the opportunity to create new visions merely because the working modalities of the tool were totally different from any other previous or existing art medium. To attempt to make "art" required the artist to invent a totally different approach.

The startup digital years were dedicated to simulating other media appearances (such as paint, charcoal, pastels, watercolor and graphite). The challenge back then was to push the limited graphic capabilities of first generation PCs to demonstrate art intent by displaying user sensitivity to other media - electronically. The work was successful if, to the eye, the pixels clusters convincingly appeared to bleed like paint. Fail to do this left the imagery with a telltale, stereotypical, computer graphics appearance. Glitz that sparkled somewhat like Opt Art but sterile due to the absence of warmth from a sense of the human touch. Thus my earlier involvement as painter and sculptor directed my approach on the computer. I "pushed and pulled" pixels to create visual sensations of traditional art media, thereby seeking validation of such digital imagery as fine art.

Such a digital goal is once removed from creating directly on canvas or in stone. A masterful manipulation of physical material creates successful stand-alone objects of art. But now, using similar sensitivity to mimic the traditional media on the computer results in creating instead an illusion of the abstract object. It's not really paint or stone. Imagery is not built to maintain the intrinsic visual quality of the medium, here the photonic dots. Instead the pixels are manipulated to become referent to some other physical mat-

ter. Art's presence is sensed by pixels becoming a *representation* of
something else other than its physical electronic self.

Luckily today composing pixels to look like real art materials
is now only a secondary concern for me. Today's hardware and
software make this challenge of yesterday almost effortless. Years
ago I had to struggle to make electronic pictures appear as art,
to feel like art. Today sophisticated software, like Fractal Painter,
oozes the look of paint straight out of the box. No personal software adjustments are necessary to get the medium crossover right.
Mimicry is guaranteed by the default values set by the programmer. Suddenly everybody's works looks more convincingly artistic,
but at the expense of a convergence of everybody's work towards a
common fine arts solution. The most overheard question among
digital artists at show openings is "What program did you use?"

Liberated from the chore to work at making convincing aesthetic marks, I can now focus more effort on inventing new visionary worlds. The computer is a powerful tool that can lead me
to discover unique imagery impossible with other art media. With
my since adopted psychology and philosophy for making art, my
intent is to produce new sensations that trigger new experience,
even awareness of the self, for the spectator. With the focus of
kindling aesthetic experience rather than object making and with
intended display in online virtual space (and the image stays at
home on the monitor) instead of on real gallery walls, the computer has evolved for me the artist into merely a tool among other
media choices, enabling me to visualize for others whatever I can
successfully imagine.

Falling Through Portal 2000

November 22, 1999

Here we are in the bottom of the ninth of the 20th century, with the top of the first of 2000 up to bat. Let me for a moment pitch a glimpse of the future.

We as a global civilization embark into a wonderous world of new high technology, unimaginable even to us living with the products and services already provided by existing technology. Airplanes, automobiles, satellites, telephones, television, computers, cell phones and now the Internet are only the preparation for what our world will be like in the next millennium. It is great to be a child today and have a lifetime to reap the benefits of past generations' ingenuity in making our lives more productive, healthy and enjoyable.

Already those that can afford it can already access the Internet in their palm, without any encumbering wiring. The global networking of the Internet is invading our television sets. We will also soon be able to dial up a Web site on your telephone, or talk to others as if on the telephone through the Internet. The first decade of the second millennium will see accelerated integration of technologies packaged into multi-purpose gadetry. The best of older technology will be bundled with new invented applications while former products and services may be laid to rest as their usefulness are rendered obsolete by new strategies that combine such functions with next generation technology.

What does all this mean for digital art? I foresee the day when as consumers we can "hang" electronic imagery on our walls! We can go out to the department store and purchase affordable "frames," derivations evolved from flat screen computer monitor technology. Such "imagers" would have the minimum memory necessary to merely display graphic files from inserted disks or CDs, thereby keeping price down. The "imager" shall also be able to be project digitized imagery to the opposing wall and at whatever size best serves interior design preferences. Then there can be the ultra cool option of a Minimalist "invisible frame." The frame is receded into the wall, and when off, the viewing surfaces convincingly matches the surrounding wall. No more distracting picture framing!

Maybe by then we won't even need disks and CDs. Imagine imagery by favorite artists that can be accessed through suscription via satellites that transmit to such intelligent picture frames, ever ready to receive such wireless visual data. Upon seeing such "on approval," suscribers can click "Save" what they like, inserting work into the personal "collection" via an automatic billing system of the networked art marketing enterprise. Actual "brick and mortar" paintings and framed posters and prints will have to compete for this consumer wall space. The present commercial art market will be thrown into a state of flux. Possibly after this transitory period, the only paintings left hundreds of years from now will be those preserved in museums. By then everything in the household may be electronic. Except our art? I don't think so!

Think about the diversity of evolving display possibilities for fine art products of the future society. Solar panels hung on external residential walls provide free power to display inside electronic imagery. Incoming visual data turns on signal sensitive frames automatically. Images change over time, set by the user's preferred rate of change. Include speakers in the frame so sound can enhance a multi-media experience in such fine arts. Wake up to sounds and images from an adapted clock-in-a-frame. On and on, creative solutions to enjoying art digitally is endless. After we arrive at this juncture, we will all laugh at the near-sightedness of much of the art world of today who resist the acceptance of digital art as fine art. Then there is the prophetized holographic 3-D sculptural imagery that can add virtual fantasy as needed in the living room through popular pricing. Realization then too will be that this digitally based baseless (no pedestal needed) form is "sculpture," or simply art.

Eventually the Internet won't be constrasted as a dichotomy with the physical world as it is today.It will be a part of our unifed experience of living, the functions it serves seamlessly mediated into our other conveniences of modern life. The world as we know it, especially in reference to our fine art and cultural heritage, will always remain within our collectic memory and cultural depositories, such as the museums. But today's reality always becomes tomorrow's history and we have no choice but to participate in man's journey, destined towards new future realms of existence. This includes art.

We Cyberartists Have a Pipedream

We Cyberartists have a pipe dream. Through our art, best fitted to the digital network that the spidery Web is, we pipeline our "cyber"-works for "cyber"-culture's sake that is globally prevalent. When I first established a presence on line for my "Truly Virtual Web Art Museum" in 1997, I had difficulty finding good digital art online to fill the virtual gallery spaces with international computer art. It was pretty much a vast e-wasteland. But it held the promise that scores of digital artists would soon arrive to claim this new realm of art opportunity.

And yes, today, they pervasively inhabit this exciting, proliferating cyberspace! There is now such a diverse richness online of cyberarts that I am proud to be part of this pioneering first generation of artists that are providing culture unique to the Web.

"Cyberart," according to my thinking and mission, is digital art that is created exclusively for viewing, appreciation, and experiencing, on the Internet. Imagine the power to now be able to share your feelings, ideas, as artist with anybody on the planet, bypassing the bottlenecks that museums and galleries are, in the democratic distribution of art for public visibility. All one has to do is conform to the medium of expression that best fits this electronic modality, the computer, the network, the boxy screen. Not all artists, especially the sculptors, take naturally to this beckoning new art medium. But for me, like a fish to water, it was a natural extension from "computer artist" (1985-96) to "cyberartist" (1997- present). It just took a change of commitment from printing-framing-nailing-hanging-on-the-wall to merely uploading new works to my web pages.

Now a new milestone for all cyberartists - the EHCC World Tour of cyberartists, disciples for the new art only visible on the Internet - now downloaded, printed out, to reveal themselves to those who only see in the "real world"- outside the inner space of online existence. Hopefully this will open eyes and show more the path to the hidden dimension of new art just a fingertip away, lying buried, like hidden treasures, on their desktops.

Statement for Pipedreams exhibition at Lincoln Center, New York, NY by Dr. Rodney Chang, curator of cyberart EHCC traveling show with group's work invited into Pipedreams as one entry; exhibition organized by Judith Wray of valweb.org; January 2002

Rodney E. J. Chang

2003 Digital Art to Painting Considerations
Pygoya Digitals to Oils

In much of my new digital art, texture is very important. The digital image is simulated to look like it is art on a canvas background. The layered canvas weave fiber pattern is important in making the eye see and think of canvas based painting, not digital light imaging.

In producing a real painting from the original digital design, it is important not to lose the canvas pattern and feeling of texture under the paint.

The perfect reproduction would be to actually paint by hand the digital canvas fiber pattern simulation. If photographs of the painted reproduction are inspected side by side, the painted canvas copy cannot be chosen from the two photographs. They would look exactly alike.

Now if painting the canvas is too difficult, then maybe the next best solution, to keep the original digital art look of simulated or artificial canvas, is to use extra rough or coarse canvas material. Or maybe use unprimed canvas to maintain rough canvas texture. Another possible approach is to paint in thin layers, not thick paint that block out the underlying canvas texture.

My digital painting simulations also have program-applied simulation of brushwork and thicker edges of paint for the artificial brush strokes. For reproduction of the image, the real brush must also have thicker edges of paint from the brush, copying exactly the digital brush stroke and uneven paint layering or distribution off the brush.

The painter must also be aware of the lighting simulation of the surface of the digital simulated painting. Sometimes it will appear like the light is shining on the digital paint surface from the side, top, or even from the bottom of the image. Such artificial digital lighting applied from software helps create the believability of the existence of a real material surface.

Therefore, in summary, extreme faithfulness in reproduction of the digital into a real painting must have diligent copying of all these simulated painter effects, so important to Pygoya cyberart.

Inspection of initial paintings by new craftsman-painters follow the above guidelines in order for the digital designer to critique successful execution of digital-to-paint reproduction.

Later, May 25, 2003 –

I'm dazed over the beautiful "copy, reproduction, human 'Paint Out II' results (did Paintout I series in 1985-1997). With such quality, there is no controversy whether they are "fine art" objects or not. But there is subsequent controversy about who is the artist, now not whether it is the computer or the user, but if it is the painter or the digital designer.

Perhaps it is merely academic, a problem of the art world that labels for pricing and gives recognition to the makers. I believe that in the business world, all that is desired and paid for with a large purchase is the object, the big impressive and sensual object. Once such is acquired by a corporation, the work contributes to the company's own image of power and the public perception of the firm's patronage and acculturation into contemporary high tech culture.

Imagine, as the Beatles sang, a legion of cloned images from such made-by-hand paintings, born from digital parentage, as nicely selling prints (Epson 2000s or Giclees), second generation (from the painted rendition and not the original digital file) that further blur the distinction, the boundary, between digital art and traditional art, by substituting the paintbrush for the pixel.

For those so compelled, squint as they must, they will scratch their heads in confusion as they try to discern the pixel, aware that they are looking at something painterly, yet oddly computerish. Still disturbed by unresolved curiosity, they, after close observation, are compelled to step back once again and merely enjoy "seeing" truly new (and thereby historic) works of art, no matter where they came from or "who dun it."

Rodney E. J. Chang

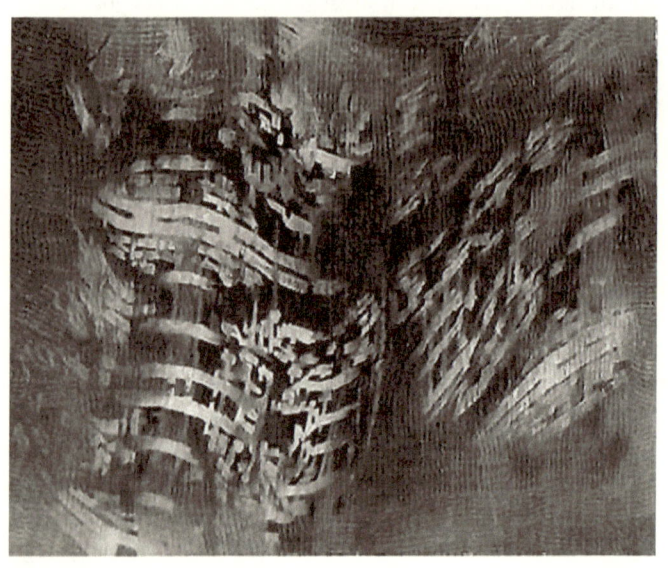

Bamboo Connection
- example of significance of simulated canvas texture for painting copist

Online Manifesto of Webism

Webists consider themselves free spirits who create for all mankind with the hope to promote understanding and harmony among all men. Noble goals for idealistic artists. - Larry Lovett (M.S.Ed., Columbia University)

Pygoya, October 2003

1. Creates art using any medium to share primarily online and thereby contribute to and expand Cyberculture

2. Contribute digital art, as a product of the same technology that makes the Internet a reality, as the main source for global cyberculture

3. Network artists together with the mission of building Web visual arts culture

4. Promote a sense of the peace through friendship without barriers and expand global consciousness

5. Identify this new specialized form and application of digital art/graphics (monitor size presentation, what- you-see on screen is the 'original' work of art, web page/site environment for the imagery, inclusion even of mixed media elements through high tech tools)

6. Demonstrate the existence of identifiable personal styles among the developed digital artists.

7. Recognize those artists that deserve the world's recognition for excellence within their chosen medium, even if not yet so by the traditional art establishment/market and their critics.

8. Declare the ephemeral digital online image as the original work of art when displayed in the cyberspace of the Internet.

9. Organize exhibitions online to showcase talent of the artists and the expressive and cognitive statements the works themselves generate

10. Document the activities of the Webists as they unite to form a new worldwide -ism in Art; record their existence and passing for traditional historians to discover thereafter

11. Organize off line exhibits to expand the awareness of more people (both lay public and art institutions) of different regions and cultures of the world of the existence of the Webist movement

12. Assist off line digital artists in the acceptance of their art tools as a legitimate fine arts medium

13. Distinguish for the public the differences in meaning of "graphic artist," "digital artist, "cyberartist," and "Webist."

14. Create opportunities where Webists can physically meet each other, outside of cyberspace and the limitation of email

15. Create and promote an identity of a new group of artists with such common goals as a historic art movement, here conceived and materialized through the new communication modality of the World Wide Web

16. Educate through awareness, the next generation in the schools, of the new generation of digital art available a click away on their computers; try to teach the ethic of not stealing online copyrighted works of art

17. Promote the marketability of signed limited edition prints as worthy commodities to help support Web artists efforts online

Digital Printmaking: A Webist's Perspective

Pygoya, Founder of Webism, October 2003

Like life itself, time flies for an artist working with digital tools. Yet despite the startup availability of the personal computer graphic platform almost twenty years ago (1984, the IBM XT/ Lumina software), digital art as an art form still is generally perceived to be a "new" and "emerging" (not fully accepted) medium. I did guess back in the mid-80s that "things would be different" 10 years later through the efforts of the first wave or generation of digital artists. Well here we pioneers are, 18 years after that prediction, working together with a vastly enlarge pool of digital artists of the second generation. Not just ubiquitous efforts from around the globe, as evidenced by the digital art that populates the Internet, but works much more sophisticated than efforts of the earlier epoch through the advancement of high technology.

Well how far have we come, given the passage of almost two decades? Unfortunately, digital art still has not found its patrons; it remains a tough sell. I am acquainted with talented cyberartists that produce developed works imbibed with personal style, abroad as well as locally, yet everyone complains about minimal sales. But I remain committed to the belief that our time of prosperity will come. Noticeably, some great pioneers have passed on without proper reimbursement for their creative sacrifices, such as Canadian living legend Robert Downing. Yet like any other type artist, we digital ones continue to explore the medium's potentials, not so much for the money but because of the internal drive and conviction within. We all keep making the most of our God given talents and maintain the dream of a future with social recognition and financial redemption. Ah, to be "rich and famous" someday continues to allure otherwise rational folks into becoming artists.

Besides the enrichment of visual effects in contemporary digital work, high technology has contributed to other aspects of fine art, including the resilient traditional art market. Nowadays it's commonplace to see signed and limited edition Giclée prints, or, the high end of computer printouts. Whereas such a product was considered 'reproductions' of 'original art,' today they are accepted as print editions, or valuable commodities, in their own right. One large Giclée in a local Honolulu frame shop recently sold for $3,000, with the help of an extra fancy wooden frame job. The artist numbered it as part of a 150 print edition. Amazingly, the image was merely a photograph of the original photorealistic rendering in oil of a pod of coconuts, in other words, an imitation copy (printed on canvas cloth with simulated brush stroke varnishing) of a painting. I had to examine up close to identify it as a print instead of a hand painted work of art. At a normal viewing distance, the print mimics an actual painting. Imagine how much the painting itself must fetch!

But is this 'original' oil on canvas worth it? Apart from how famous this particular artist is and his specific technical skills with paint manipulation, the work is more or less a copy of nature, here, some coconuts. So when it comes to the concept of originality, the painting, like most landscapes aiming for photorealism, is a rip off of nature, a reproduction of it. This genre of paintings is illusions to convenient bring nature inside one's living space. So a derived Giclée is a copy of a copy. Compare this to digital art conceived by the artistic mind through the vehicle of software tools where there is no original physical complement to the printout. In my mind a Giclée of this venue is a true original work of art, as no physical precedent exists before the virtual picture's materialization into a tangible image on paper.

Besides the high end Giclée, cyberartists can now turn to the more affordable Epson 2000 series print with archival "watercolor" paper and inks. These are as collectible as any other type of printmaking if the manufacturer's claim of 200 years of no fading of their inks holds up to the test of time. Despite this supremacy of original digital imagery for the Giclée process, as a Webist who creates virtual (digital) imagery for Internet online display, I declare my paper prints, Giclée or Epson, for what they are - 'reproductions' of the ephemeral digital art. Of course the signature on prints are hand signed. In fact my personal preference for 'output' of the digital image is the execution of oil on canvas paintings. This caters to the mystique of painting and its perceived collectibility, even if in essence the one-of-a-kind work of art is a derivative (of the digital domain).

Technology offers other art product end products unique to digital art. These include today's CDs and DVDs. Besides 'slide shows' or more elaborate animation of still digital images, the pictorial can be combined with music and other multimedia elements to create a new 'mixed media' specific for this electronic age and its sensitivities.

My prediction for our newborn and fledging digital art? Technology will continue to shape the way we create *all* art. For example, innovations in glass blowing, metal casting, and ceramics through electronic advancement in equipment and materials, the modernization of art supply production such as synthetic acrylic paints, and the emergence of digital cameras and photographic enhancements and print processing. In the short term the digital will continue to integrate with all forms of artistic creation. In the intermediate term I have no doubt that the digital medium will reign supreme as the epoch's dominant medium to depict cultural identity. Not just regionally, but globally, as witnessed by the rapidly expanding influence of global Internet cyberculture that catapults all geographical borders. Then a time will come when the cultural digital mainstream will be shocked by a young underground revolting against the establishment by reviving hand crafted artwork. Such works, judged primitive by nature in an overwhelming social environment embedded in technology, will have a difficult time standing up to critical ridicule, just as we early cyberists have had to and still endure.

Mouse Mightier than the Brush

- A blog prepared for and published at absolutearts.com on October 22, 2004)

Digital art visualizes abstract science. The working e-artist always knows there is a precise mathematical base concealed within the patterns of chromatic pixels of light. Yet, instead of highlighting the math behind the art, most digital artists select to merely apply the power of the medium to express their own subjective view and feeling of life. The digital image "works" if it induces an emotional or harmonic resonance within the artist who orchestrates the composition.

Such quantifiable and dissecting precision of art data leads to cloned mixtures of previous digital images that formulate subsequent new work derivatives. Such serial shuffling of clustered pixels become the visual markers of one's style. Cutting & pasting, stacking images into layered transparencies, morphing with distortion tools, themselves all raw works in process, lead to the completed piece that personifies. In a sense, the artist's repertoire of works have common genetic art traits that continually get reworked, remixed, reinvestigated, spliced & diced into new wholes, all with an evolving skill for efficiency that includes aesthetic control of visual redundancy.

Taking this refined digital art unto the Internet stage forces the artist to consider the social context in which the work is unveiled. The presentation parameters and audience reach are quite different from the traditional "brick and mortar" exhibition. Virtual show information retrieved from search engines replaces the formal invitation snail-mailed only to the privileged. Art embedded in HTML may be perpetually accessible, ending the regrets of missing "brick and mortar" openings and closings. Mature e-art may eventually include elements in the work that provide credence of intention for the art to be experienced exclusively online. This function and unique platform for display distinguishes Web art from the broader category of "digital art," limited to archival, signed and limited printout. A group could evolve that provides original art in such a new context, adding substance to its content.

An early declaration of this mission for art is the current Webists with their manifesto for Webism. Through sharing ideas, initiating global meetings (and sipping wine together), networking for interactive projects, advancing a body of works under the banner of a new 'ism as declared by the pioneering artists, a truly new body of works may take root in this vast and nebulous cyberplace called the Web. Web-art might even provide a new channel for people of the world to communicate, share ideas, and nurture fellowship that liberates one from physical solitaire and in-grained nationalism.

Webism could counteract the present "brick and mortar" museum fragmentation into special interest institutions, each splintering restricting collections to the promotion in value of their own cultural artifacts, ignored or underrepresented by the more prominent museums. Surfing online may lead to stumbling upon the more ubiquitous cyberart which could enrich the lives of millions around the planet, many who can only draw a straight line (even digitally)) with the assistance of Paint Box. Online virtual art may well be the **only** art some will ever see in their culturally deprived real life situation. Hopefully, even without a formal art education, those that do search can see the universal spirituality of all mankind shine through the digital.

Visions of Sugar Plums Dancing in Their Heads for Art's Sake

Eve of December 24, 2004
A presentation to Downtown Initiative for the Visual Arts when Pygoya
visits Eugene, Oregon and meets DIVA's Executive Director,
Mary Unruh

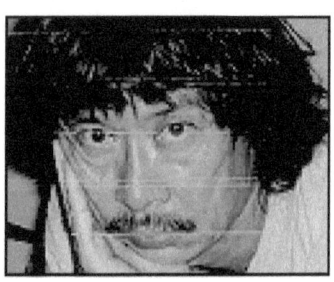

I once did preliminary study of comparing art preferences of individuals while conscious or in the hypnotic trance. Although inconclusive, there seems to be the possibility that the art style we prefer in the conscious state may differ from what we prefer in a less self-awareness state, such as the hypnotic trance. Strange? What's going on here? Do we deceive ourselves when we buy art that we "like" for our homes or select unaware that our choices are conditioned by social and cultural guidelines? For example, even if one covertly lusts for a pornographic work of art, would it be bought and hung in a Christian home where Bible study meetings are held? Is it not more socially acceptable to buy a generic landscape that simply mirrors the local region? The strongest local art market is for landscapes of palm trees and beaches in Hawaii, golden yellow and red trees of autumn in Oregon, desert cactus and Spanish stucco dwellings in New Mexico, and Cape Cod cottage waterfronts in New England.

I thought of my past effort to research art appreciation when I read an article in today's morning paper, "Study links dreams to sleep stages." This latest sleep research demonstrates that the first couple of hours of REM are dominated with **emotionally charged**, even aggressive, dreams. The subsequent latter six or so hours of the normal sleep cycle are characterized with more "friendly, unthreatening dreams." According to lead researcher Patrick McNamara, professor of neurology at Boston University School of Medicine, these socially aggressive dreams were never found to occur during non-REM sleep throughout the entire study. The study was limited to 15 sleeping college students. The hypothesis presented for such results is that if the brain is organizing dreams in a purposeful way, then the emotional and social oriented dreams might "constrain, shape, modulate or influence the number and types of interactions that you're going to engage in during the day to come." I do remember the times, during periods of conflict with past significant others, that dreaming was dominated with the disturbing angst of life's moment; it was if I couldn't get the problem out of my mind, no escape even when I slept. 24/7.

I see also some implications of this new dream research when it comes to understanding art appreciation. For an artist like myself, this dream study results support my approach to deliberate inclusion of psychological content within my manipulated works of art.

The hypnotic trance seems to overlap daydreaming during the conscious state. Should the teacher reprimand that child in the classroom for not paying attention or permit him or her to continue to look out the window and daydream, possibly learning in an alternative manner? We artists tend to daydream a lot as young students. My chronic inattentiveness in class resulted in teachers' denigration in the commentary section of my report cards, to the chagrin of my worried parents. In spite of it all I grew up to be a well-adjusted artist.

It would be interesting to study the relationships between daydreaming and the almost trance-like mental mode artists work in when completely involved during the creative process. It is a great experience to lose one's self in one's art and become one with the piece under development. There is a satisfying sense of accomplishment when a completed work mirrors personal emotional expression, making tangible for others the artist's inner self. Then there have been times that I fortuitously was able to wake myself up to capture images I saw in the dream. So just what are the correlations among dreams, daydreams, and the artist's trance-like creative process?

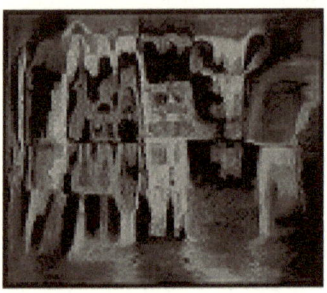

I believe there are different levels of human consciousness. When we transition from awake to sleep, we pass through the stages of daydreaming, then the realm of the hypnotic, before entering the dream world of REM, and subsequent non-REM deep, almost vegetative state of sleep. To awaken we travel through the reverse order of cerebral stations. Based upon this theory of ordered psychological states, I intentionally load my own artwork, superficially labeled "abstract," with subliminal and emotive visual elements. The depth that I seek to elicit from the even casual viewer goes beyond what they consciously discern to comprehend. To go beyond this initial instinctive effort to identify just what they are confronting as abstract art, is superfluous visual content laden with symbolic triggers that excite the unconscious realm of the mind, not unlike the insightful postulations of the psychologist Carl Jung.

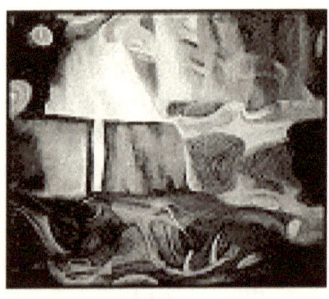

Can art be significant because it is more effective than the mundane objects of our daily life in enabling us to tap areas of our brain not utilized in our normal awaken state? For example, the passion felt when looking at "great art" that is as intense as the emotions we experience in the REM dream state? How many times have we heard people say at art shows, simultaneously defensively and defiantly, "I don't understand art but I KNOW WHAT I LIKE." Is ignorance, in fact, bliss? Or is art a catalyst that assists us to day "dream" while awake, thereby connecting into the Jungian herd "Universal Unconscious?"

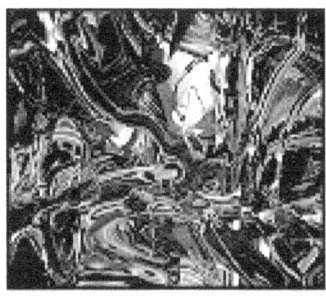

I am convinced that my work's attraction goes beyond competent control of formal composition - line, rhythm, color harmony, balance, varied distribution of shapes and depth, etc., but intrigue because I intentional attempt to rig the design with metaphoric ambiguity. This supplemental content, at first hidden, exerts its presence after the initial interpretation of the work. The viewer can be led to see is such a way through a guiding title for the abstract, such as "Black Forest," "Dancing Fumes," and "Sailing in Cyberspace." But I believe visual interest is prolonged by incorporation of subtle details with unconscious symbolic significance. Such esoteric, unaware associations by the viewer assist in personalizing the relationship with the encountered work of art. It makes them feel oddly anew, establishes a connection they don't quite understand, creates an interest that mystifies, targeting the urge to bond and possess. Pretty landscape, move over!

Rodney E. J. Chang

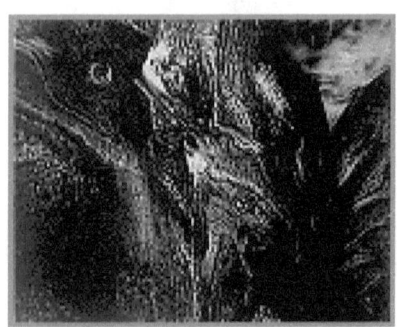

Beyond Cosmetic Dentistry
or Stuck Between a Rock and a Hard Place

(Invited submittance for the Hawaii Dental Association Journal,
November 2004 issue)

Rodney "Pygoya" Chang,
(reference bio - www.lastplace.com/page28.htm)

I am an individual stuck between two worlds. I here am not referring to the gray area that I emotionally reside in between the two professions that I practice, that of dentistry and fine arts. Instead I acknowledge the rugged path I have chosen, making nebulous wares that exist somewhere between traditional fine art and the more theoretical realm of aesthetics. Artists do not take naturally to an analytical approach that describes what they make and who they are. They shun psychology, realizing that the hardship of being a "starving artist," even with worthy works, can land them on a psychiatrist's couch. Like the patient that changes dentist, artists hate rejection and blame others for not understanding their work.

When I was in art graduate school, I questioned why I was, in orthodox fashion, nurtured to copy the current contemporary fads in painting. I was not allowed to create my own icons from scratch, but was directed to adhere to what had already been condoned as "significant" art by critics and historians. I asked my clinical, I mean studio, instructor about his opinion on some of the ideas expressed in a book on "beauty" that I was reading - outside of class. He warned me, "Don't think so much, **just paint!** ("If you want to graduate on time"). After that exchange I was convinced I had to get off the beaten path to becoming a professional artist via the Master of Fine Arts credentialing process. I did stick around long enough to earn my Masters of Art in Studio Art (Northern Illinois University, 1975) before exploring art theory and aesthetics through a self-directed doctorate program (Union Graduate Institute, 1980).

My redirected academic pursuit, possibly empowered from post-traumatic left-brain stimulation of dental school (and degrees in psychology to better understand my future patients and myself), led me to explore art in the psychological, philosophical, and sociological disciplines. I spent four time consuming but glorious years to answer for myself - "What is Art? What is Beauty?" - before embarking on my lifelong practice of art production. During those developmental years, I was fortuitous to have established a personal art theory and philosophy as *modus operandi* in the search for hidden new imagery. This working model for making my idiosyncratic visual statements provides reassurance of aesthetic value, a rationale for artistic decision making for works in process, and a theoretical defense against criticism levied by authority attacking with obsolescent criteria and subjective biases. Let me explain how I am deviant from the complying conventional artist.

I use CAD or 3D computer modeling. I would prefer to be using artificial intelligence but no program exists for fine arts application - yet. I am team oriented. I conduct virtual staff meetings via the Internet, provide leadership and take final responsibility for results. I prep the virtual object, then not unlike taking an impression and sending it out (a printout and digital graphic file), delegate an art technician to fabricate the work. A painting takes months to painstakingly simulate the digital original. I in turn make the adjustments, and then deliver the work to the "patient" (the art client). The painting is evaluated for specifications prescribed to the craftsmen. I only use the best art lab, having changed several times when quality is unsatisfactory. There is no 'redo' in this process. Faithful reproduction without the highest quality would hurt my reputation. Most damaging of all, the virtual art made tangible, and collectible, would then not be my own work but a hack misinterpretation of my vision. From this characterized work process you can understand how my philosophy as aesthetician differs from the conventional artist-craftsman. I sign paintings executed from digital images sent out to the lab of master copyists. I affectionately call them my "human printers."

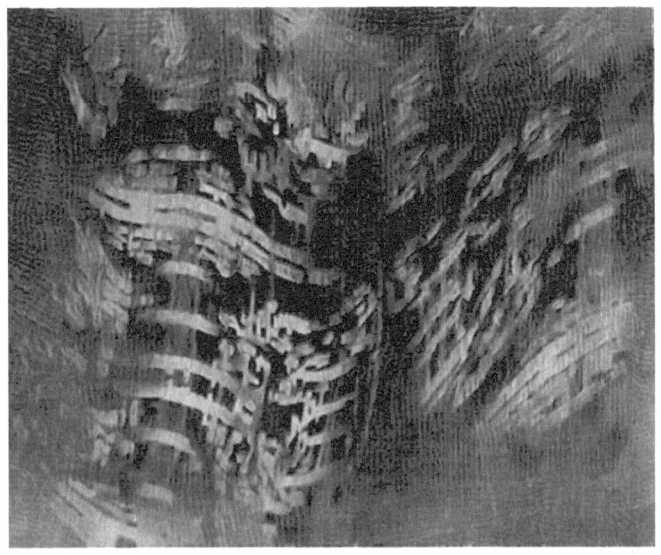

Bamboo Rain Forest, oil on canvas, 2003

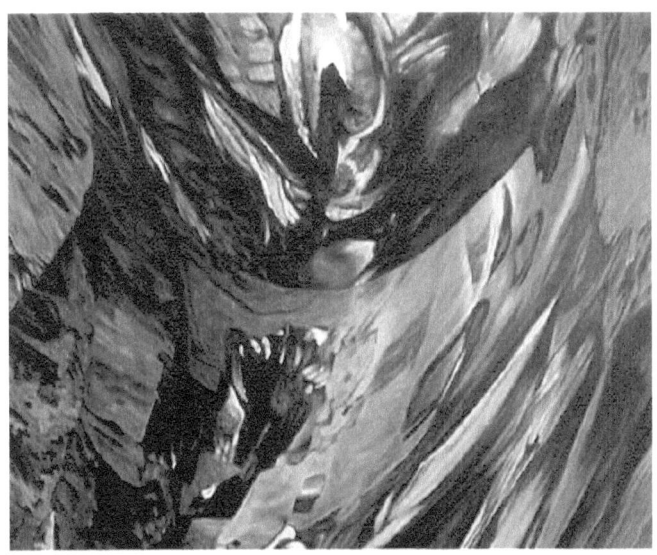

Heat Rap, oil on canvas, 2003

I don't label myself as an "artist" but view myself as a specialist in "visionary painting design" - which nobody in the art business understands. I take this to be evidence that I am, like so many have proclaimed, "ahead of my time" as an art practitioner, or in other words, will "become famous after I am dead." *(Sales pitch: buy one now for your reception room and write it off!)* I apply psychological principles and strategies into my abstract art when other abstractionists cop out, giving total credence of their visual expression to their "feelings," dubious to themselves due to a lack of background in psychology. I openly state I know more about what my art **means** (and what it evokes from my targeted audience) than most professional art critics and writers who, when pressed to write about my work, inevitably getting it wrong. Especially those adamant to fight back and defend dated "modern art" from the onslaught of today's digital art revolution. I divorced myself from my earlier years of painting, sculpture, ceramics, photography, mixed media (used dental anesthetic carpules in one work of art), and art installations (the famous one being "Da Waiting Room," my former disco dental clinic featured on world TV). I look back at this flirtation period with different media as internships before deciding to specialize in digital art. I enjoy leading the crusade of digital image processing, the globally despised and feared imagery that democratizes art, taking away the monopoly of making pictures away from artists. Now anybody can claim to be an artist with the crutch of a computer. Of course a lot of garbage as output confounds the public, giving the medium a black eye.

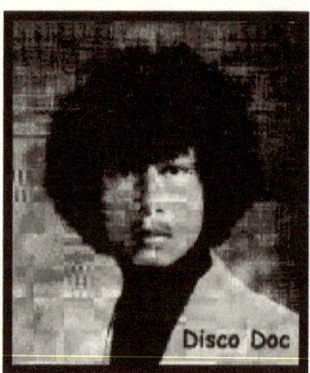

Disco Doc on NBC's Real People, 1979

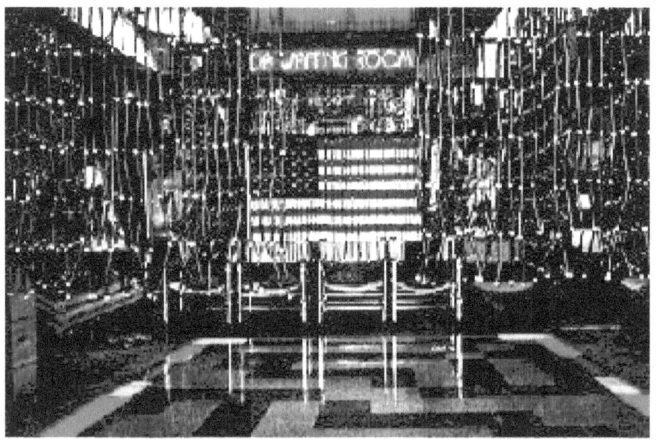

Da Waiting Room clinic reception area, 1979-1996

But I come into the field grounded in visual aesthetics, psychology, art history, and yes, with a sense of cosmetic dentistry and design functionality, all coupled to the mission of expanding the boundaries of art, or just what can be visually piqued on the monitors of PCs (since their arrival in the 1980s). Indeed, my high speed brush has enabled me to visualize the unforeseen, original paintings that could have never been conceived with mere paint laden bristles on a stick. The banter of whether digital art is collectible or even "art" is as obscure to my consciousness as the developed tinnitus in my ears from decades of high-speed turbines (and yes, blasting disco dance clubs - By the way, I still dance at **Rumors** in Waikiki on occasional Saturday nights when I run a fever). I remain focused to the dedication of producing fresh new imagery, either as original oil paintings on canvas (although I do not directly "paint" them; I also don't do my own lab work), **Giclee'** print knock offs, or the actual "original" digital files uploaded onto my Internet virtual art museum (www.lastplace.com). Like a diligent doctor, I document all my work in writing and keep good records and art progress reports in my online journal (www.lastplace.com/page49.htm).

Rodney E. J. Chang

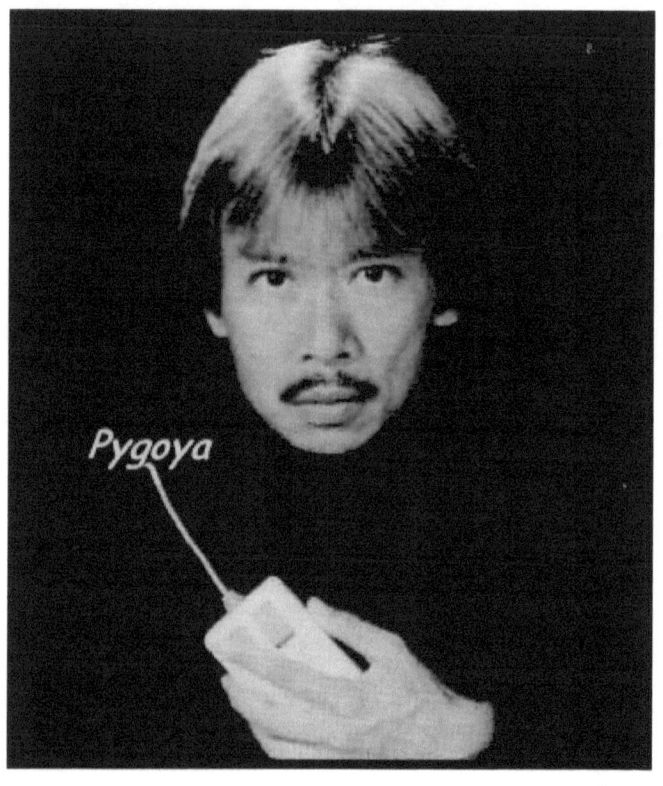

Pygoya at Shanghai Museum, 1985

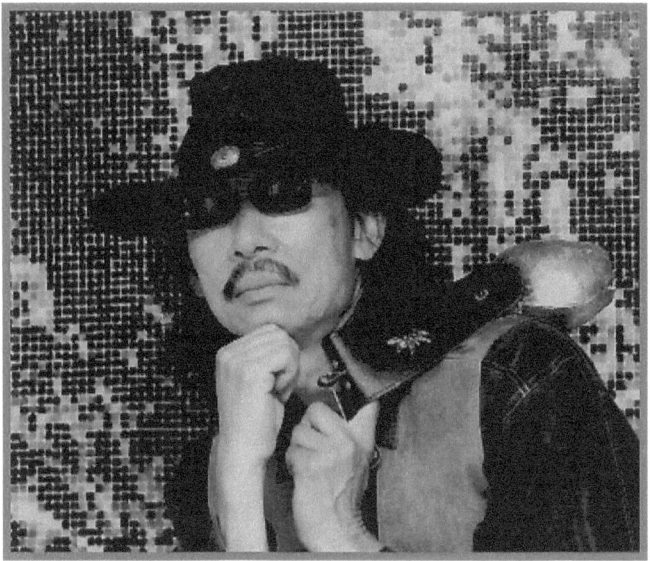

Pygoya on tour in Paris, Frankfurt, Budapest & Vienna, 2003

As an artist I care less about authorship than taking on the role of catalyst to manifest innovative works of art to behold. If I am the father, the computer is the mother. Artists around the globe consider me the "founder of Webism" (www.artingrid.de). Without this cybernetic painting tool, the body of works I have accomplished and will continue to wean outside of the box of mainstream art could never materialize. I am satisfied as an artist; I am lucky to have found my medium, and thereby myself, through and in my works. This adjustment makes me a more content dental clinician.

Rodney E. J. Chang

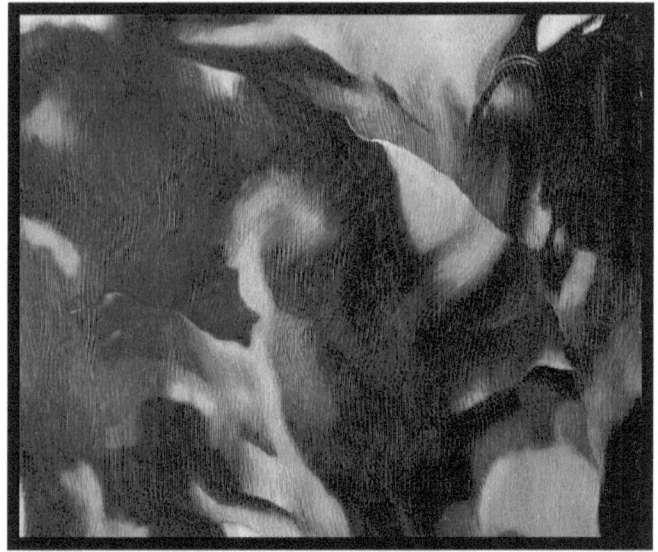

Dancing Red Dress, oil on canvas, 2004

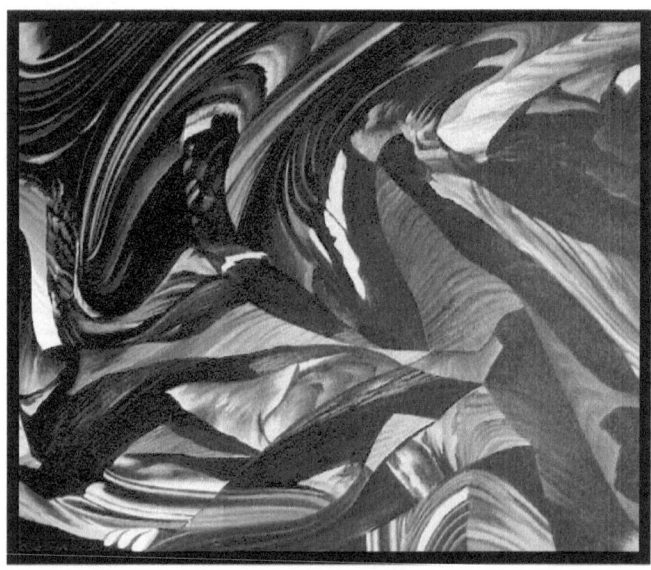

Quake, oil on canvas, 2004

Like a dentist, I work to provide a life enriching service to the public. Through dentistry and art, I have a double challenge as ***provider***. I am a health professional but also a cultural change agent. I task myself to create art that mirrors our increasingly digitalized selves (and dental profession!), involuntarily immersed in a society riveted to relentless, demanding technology, with an accelerating rate of evolution. Hopefully my art assists in keeping us spiritually abreast with the times. Just maybe it will be recognized historically as relevant prototypical works of the new millennium.

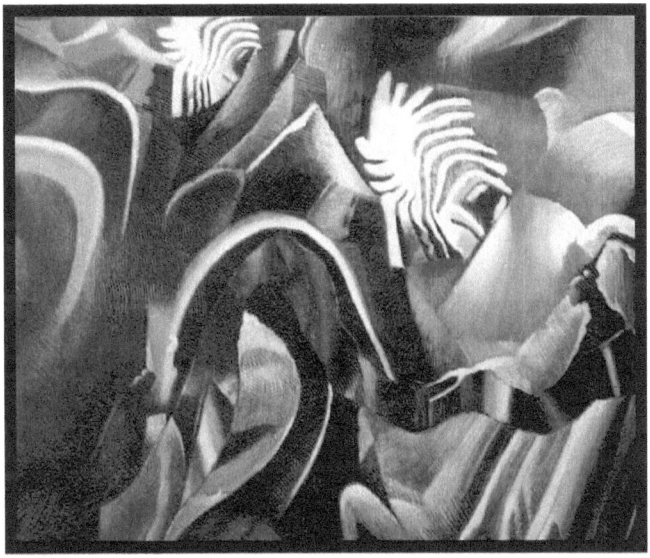

Cybergarden   2004

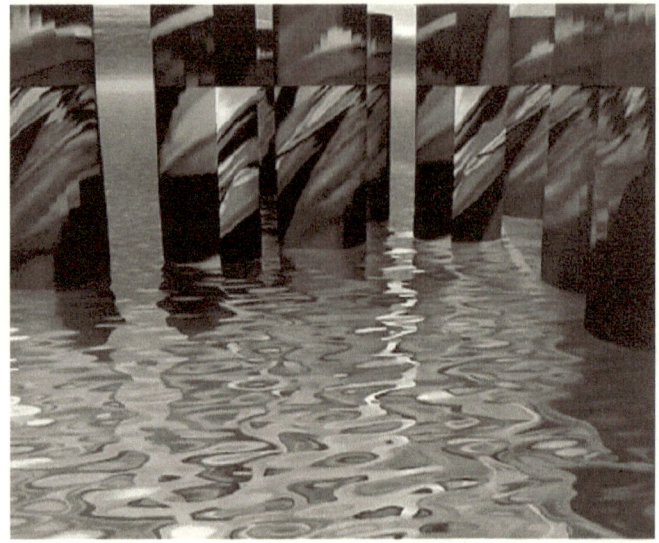

Tidal Lights 2003

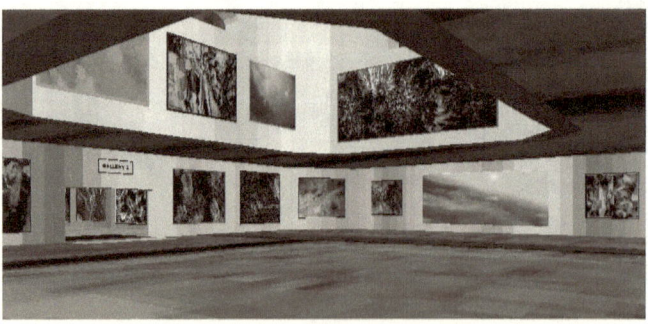

Truly Virtual Web Art Museum, www.lastplace.com

- Dr. Rodney Chang is a member of the Hawaii Dental Association and the American Society of Aesthetics. He enters his 30th year of general private practice in Kalihi. Upon retirement he looks forward to establishing an art retreat/B&B to teach aesthetic and computer graphics at Volcano on the Big Island. He also plans to continue volunteer work for the island's mobile dental care van and clinic for the Puna indigent population.

Immortality and Art

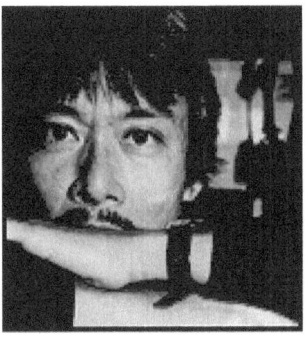

By Pygoya - an open letter to Dr. Michael Newton, author
of Journey of Souls (1994) and Destiny of Souls (2004)

Dear Dr. Newton,

With all due respect for your genius and hypnotherapy research into the spiritual world, I write this open letter of appreciation as an artist, having spent a lifetime with the conflict (and
criticism) of juggling roles and jobs in life. Your books, <u>Journey
of Souls</u> (1994) and <u>Destiny of Souls</u> (2004) help elucidate for
myself what my life has been about and assist in clarifying my
future direction in life. I now don't feel like a "lost soul" but have
identified my mission in life in the here and NOW. God willing,
I **shall** build a museum for the digital arts, with emphasis on the
Web-based type, to round out my art career. "Build it and they
shall come" will be the motto hung front and center at this im-
minent brick n' mortar institution envisioned to be located somewhere in America.

Rodney E. J. Chang

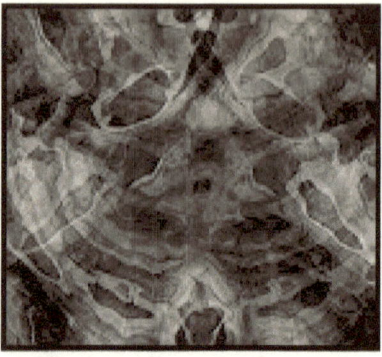

In Transit, digital

As a clinical psychologist your preferred mode of therapy is hypnosis and as an innovator you developed techniques that venture deep into not just life regression but ***between*** physical existences, ***within*** the spiritual realm. I find your work fascinating and am personally able to accept what you "report" after decades of working with clients in subconscious mental states. After all, I have used clinical hypnosis as a tool to alleviate dental anxiety as a practicing dentist, sometimes drilling painlessly even without a "shot." So there is no resistance on my part in the acceptance of your choice of research modality of the afterlife. I read your publications, with my own understanding of the power and validity of hypnosis as a means to access other levels of consciousness, with an open mind. I admire and respect your courage to publish what you have discovered.

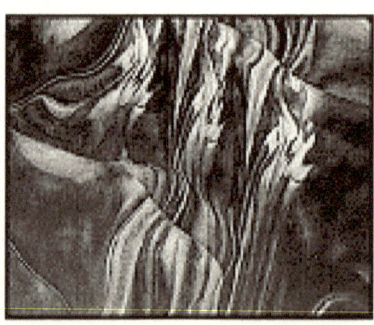

Ethereal Layers, oil on canvas

As artists we always hear "You'll be famous after you're dead (but not "rich and famous" in this life time);" "You're trying to be immortal through your art." But at 59, I have loss enough creative contemporaries to demonstrate that these clichés' are cultural myths. There has been no sudden turn around in the value of works that I have bought from the deceased after their passing. I am still stuck with a collection of local works that doesn't financially appreciate. Maybe instead of supporting my "starving artist" friends, I should have "invested" in a Picasso print 25 years ago. Of course, that really isn't the reason I acquired these works; I still derive pleasure in viewing them, and remembering the dearly departed.

And disappointingly, the attempt to achieve immortality may not be through one's effort as an artist limited to one short lifetime. It may take generations of time and effort to eventually "get to the top." I like to believe most of us are not so egocentric to selfishly believe our art isn't for the common good but also is an extension of the cultural climate that we are born into.

Even after death, quality of craftsmanship and significance of aesthetic conceptual content still counts. But besides these inherent factors that may have held back "fame and fortune" during life, there exists the definite blockages to artistic success of 1) being in the right place and time, and 2) supply and demand. As an experimental digital artist, time expended basking on the beach of Waikiki, goggling at well-packed bikinis hasn't helped. Long ago I made my life decision not to relocate to New York City after art school in Chicago but choose to return home for family sake and Hawaii's tropical "creature comforts." In regards to 2), there sure exists an abundance of talented digital artists, in plain sight on the Internet and in its cyber-cultural "global (arts) village." So many are called but very few are chosen. It's the plight of the generation of artists born into this new millennium of high technology with personal empowered visibility. There's too many of us.

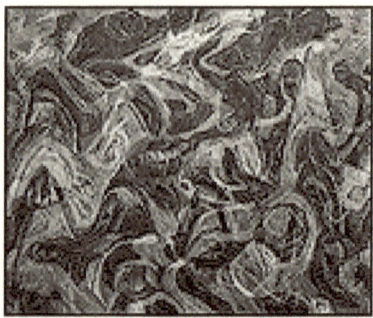

Soulful Jubilation, oil on canvas

Permit me to share how your books have been therapeutic for my life moving forward. I will get off the beach, take career risks, and move to the Mainland - where I can afford to build my own baseball diamond in the cornfields.... as in "Field of Dreams," starring Kevin Costner. I believe through the emergence of the Internet, it is feasible to "build it (anywhere, but with a great Web site) and they shall come." My extended Hawaiian vacation may be over.

I will keep stuff on "me" brief but I hope relevant as some sort of guideline for at least some artists out there, online. After all, it's doing wonders for me. I have been mobilized into action! I now have a realtor on the West Coast (USA) that specializes in commercial property, searching for museum space and I plan to take an early retirement from dentistry, as much as I like doing the work of a healer. Since we are all connected, when my private sphere reality changes, so will yours. Sometimes, as described in Malcolm Gladwell's The Tipping Point (2002), individual action can make a big difference, precipitating a sudden social change of epidemic magnitude. A museum of digital and Internet art could become a reality, no longer residing merely within one man's fanatical dream state. The Internet is the present's social context in which "Connectors," such as Ingrid Kamerbeek of the Webists, that through special personal ability brings people together. Within this new realm I like to think of myself as a "Maven," or "people who accumulate knowledge," "teach," and facilitate "word-of-mouth (social) epidemics." I use psychology to assist in our understanding of the digital medium as a unique and legitimate art form. Eventually the "Salesmen," through their Web sites, will "persuade" the mainstream of the collectibility of cyber-art, establishing quality Giclee print editions as successful commodities in the **brick n' mortar** gallery world.

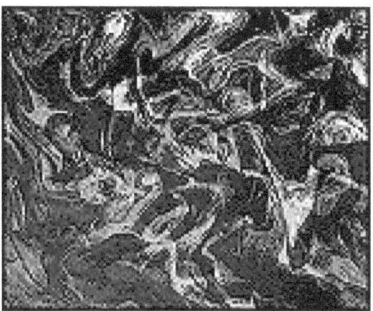

Troubled Souls, oil on canvas

Just before I read your books, Dr. Newton, available at Amazon.com and your local Barnes & Noble bookstore, I was invited to be the guest speaker at a symposium of teachers that work in the Honolulu public school gifted student program. I was "discovered" by the director through her stumbling upon my framed digital prints in a local restaurant. She declared my work to be that of a "gifted artist," thereby qualifying me to be a speaker in the educational field. Not knowing much about the specialty, I "winged it" as a "case study" documentation, with the art as validating proof for what I had to offer to these soldiers working within the trenches of limited budgeting for special education. The gifted are bunched together by the Board of Education with the unfortunates that possess "learning disabilities." Because of the economy, the local program just took a major budgetary financial hit for 2005. I consented to speak for free.

My approach for the group presentation was to do an introspective review of what it was like to be schooled in a system (1950s) where I felt like a "black sheep" unappreciated in a value system built upon the "3 Rs," providing no special support for early childhood display of artistic talent. Looking back, after having read "Journey of Souls," I now view my presentation and online journal documentation as a bit defensive for having a "multiple personality," an infliction instead of blessing from the perspective of conventional clinical psychology's models of wellness. I bought into the societal judgment that one cannot devote full dedication to managing three vocations, for me, dentistry, art, and psychology. I must be "messed up." The bottom line to my self-validating speech was that I had the energy and capacity to practice dentistry, do my art with commitment, and cope with the schizophrenic-like social criticism, all in stride to sustain personal mental health.

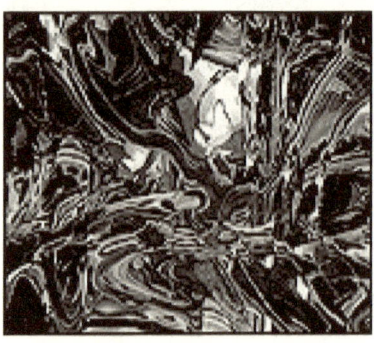

Ethereal Journey, oil on canvas

After considering what you layout, granted merely as a "reporter" of the "consistency" of description of the order of the spiritual world and reincarnations of many client-hypnotic subjects, I find it therapeutic for my own life situation. For now, thanks to your explorations, I am at peace that I *can be* a dentist as well as artist and do justice to both callings. I find the requirement of continued professional education in both fields exhilarating. I realize now that each profession has its time and place; my choices for healing *and* creating make me feel whole. I accept there is the possibility that a reincarnated artistic soul selected a dentist as supportive patron to do this specific life's bidding, a challenge for evolving during this creative life embedded within the advent of new artistic digital tools and the global communicative arena of the Internet. I recognize the synchronicity of events, that of having the financial means to establish a new *Internet Art Museum*, as well as to serve the multitude of digital artists "flagged" through the presence and discovery of their Web pages as validity of worth, both of their medium as well as personal artistic talent. I believe at this moment I am not only responsible to prove the aesthetic legitimacy of this art, of light, through my own works, but have a predestined obligation to assist in the support of the medium and its pioneering artists scattered abroad, reaching beyond the isolation of nationalism and religious camps. I stand ready, along with many others, to complete the mission.

So again, Dr. Newton, my heartfelt appreciation for clarifying what my life, my art, **is** "all about." There may be, in fact, intermediate and advanced artistic spirits now at work that specialize in an art form that exists through, and as, the vibrant energy of light itself.

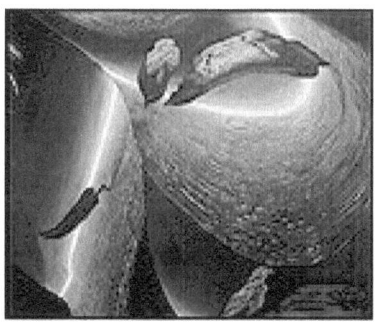

Journey of Souls, oil on canvas

With much thanks,
Pygoya

Beyond Computer Art - Part II
Pygoya, April 15, 2005

Back in 1999 I wrote how my effort as a digital artist had change since my startup in the medium in 1984. During that span of years PC hardware and software had come a long way in visualization of graphics that were more convincing as "fine art." At the beginning it was attempting to smooth out blocky pixels and jagged lines. By 1999 systems became sophisticated enough to effortlessly produce comparable airbrush quality resolution imagery. I was free to spend more creative effort in creating than editing to refine canned software marks.

Today I have the privilege to work with *Bryce* and *Vue*, powerful 3D programs. It is quite easy to capture rich visual complexity in my compositions. I can now "paint" as a professional digital artist.

I write again on what is "beyond computer art" - for me, at this juncture at 2005.

Last week I spent a day in the country at a good friend's art studio. No computer there. So, along with him, I got lost in painting with brush and canvas for 5 hours. The new works "made by hands" amaze Larry as well as myself. They represent some sort of breakthrough for me as artist. Surprisingly, the acrylic paintings appear like the digital art I now create! As I work I remember constantly referring back to step-by-step decision making that I do as a digital artist working with software and mouse. I was thinking in pixels, gradients, 3D primitives, filtering effects, etc. Even with paint my creative process and mind set was - digital!

So when the series of works successfully emulated my digital works there was this excitement that possibly, this might be a whole new style of painting. The works are abstract, a mix of Jackson Pollock and Abstract Expression in the Modernist mode. But added to the mix is the novelty of including areas that mirror 3-dimensional faceted planes and lines like those produced in 3D programs. I can't wait to create more works - without the computer.

So what, for me, is "beyond computer art?" Could I have gone 20 years applying myself to the digital medium, only to develop a painting style? Might I stop using the computer and return to painting, even sculpture, media I worked in the 70s, 80s? Have I mentally become ingrained in graphic software's aesthetic sensitivity and its mathematical manifestation through user tools that execute commands? Can I now continue to create this aesthetic WITHOUT the need to use the computer? Have I, as artist, BECOME the computer? It's all beyond me. The only elucidation of my future creative path is to keep on this path that I have chosen.

Adapting to Online Art
January 2, 2005

Not unlike the distant past, we walk into galleries and museums with a sense of reverence for the objects we behold. Like statues in a Gothic cathedral, the sculptures command a shared ceremonial appreciation that goes beyond its materialistic constitution. For many art lovers, formal exhibition space provides a supportive platform to elevate one's spiritual experience in the presence of works of art.

For Web based art there is no such ritualistic support for images downloaded unto one's monitor. No mind set for appreciating art through the portal of some architectural wonder, no fancy frames that define the enclosures of sacred paint. We instead encounter Web art in the cubicle or at a desktop. There is no tactile and ornate wooden frame but the sleek flat screen designed more for business than for admiring art. Without a set time for the unveiling of physical exhibiting through a social gathering to congratulate the artist and recognize his efforts, online art display instead is ubiquitous, tends to be anonymous, and also timeless, especially if Web pages are not updated periodically. At the expense of less social ceremony and ritual, Webism instead capitalizes on perpetual availability in one's private space and at one's convenience. It's art for the masses without the hype. It's art that bypasses parochial regionalism and affords artists the democratic opportunity to contribute to cyber-culture of the "global village."

Much of online-based art is created with the compatible digital art tools, graphic software made for fine art production. What has been the approach of programmers to construct such tools to accommodate the need of 2D artists?

On a recent trip to my Giclee' printer's workspace (Sterling Editions in Springfield, Oregon), I had the opportunity to inspect a magnificent landscape in the photo realistic style that was being reproduced as a print edition. It dawned on me that a photograph of the depicted Oregon coastal scene of lighthouse with a shoreline background would be more "realistic" than this artistic depiction of reality. Yes, I was in awe of the masterful depiction of form, surface, and detail throughout every square inch of the painting. But this is not the way our eyes see. When we focus on something in our environment, everything in the retinal foreground and background is blurry. There is limited visual "depth of field," just as in the operation of camera lenses. However here in this well crafted "photo realistic" painting, distance is suggested by the relative sizes of objects of the landscape captured on canvas. But when shifting attention around the work of art, each and every object, no matter how far it would be in the real scene from the viewer's position, was in complete focus. As such the whole picture served as an illustration of feature details of objects in the scene, not unlike a catalog documenting the physical description of things in our world. In this painting there is unrealistic clarity in the blades of grass in the foreground, bathing sunlight romanticizing aging stucco of the lighthouse tower at middle ground, and simultaneously accurate rocky detailing of the distant background mountain range. Maybe this is how a hawk sees, but definitely not the human eye.

It seems to me much of 2D digital art has more an affinity towards such photo realistic painting than it does with photography, even if both require a print for physical output. When one produces graphic marks and color from a scrolling and clicking mouse, there is this sense of working on a visual plane. Adding the simulated texture of canvas or paper as a layered background can enhance this working frame of reference. The graphic software is designed foremost to lay down shapes and colors, almost with a Modernistic train of thought whereby paint remains paint and not building blocks for creating the illusion of real life objects. Sharp edges between shapes and negative "space" are "blurred" to appear less crude to the eye. Colors are "smeared" to de-pixelate any remaining "jaggies" that give away the image's digital origins. Editing graphic commands are not labeled "foreground," "middle ground," and "background" for the convenience and needs of the landscape artist. In short, most 2D software is designed to create graphics that lie apparently on a flat surface, whether simulated artsy paper or simply on the surface of your monitor.

Along with this bias towards working with graphic software tools that are designed less for depth illusion than for imitation of paint and other traditional art medium, there is the added change of traditional visual distance between spectator and work of art. Unlike the normal separation between a painting on a museum wall and the viewer, we look at Web art close up on our desk. This space is further closed with the onset of middle age as we squint and lean forward to discern. Therefore we are inclined to inspect fine detail of virtual images, forced as if to walk close up to hung artwork, unnaturally discriminating the technical details of the surface, losing total comprehension of the overall statement of the work of art. The medium of bright monitor light also directs attention to graphic rendering skills at the expense of the more detached aesthetic sense of depth and place. Edges become more contrasting if not refined for the sake of unnaturally close visual inspection dictated by the coupled desk monitor and seated viewer confinement.

In summary, much of 2D Web digital art displays exacting graphic detail not unlike photo realistic painting. There is gravitation towards a sense of surface with universal depiction of detail down to the pixel level as opposed to effort to capture convincing illusory depth. Social gathering to ritualize the experiencing of art is replaced by private viewing without ceremony. Effort by 2D digital artists is to be make surrogate images of traditional art media under the scrutinizing overly close eye of the viewer while controlling the glare affect of emitted photons of light disguised as reflected light of paint pigment on paper or canvas. Yet as we adapt to these new requirements of the presentation of art through the portal of the Internet, new exciting visual imagery can be discovered by the spectator, more than compensating for departure from a brick and mortar art excursion.

Blink, - I Like It!
(But I don't know why)
March 1, 2005

PYGOYA

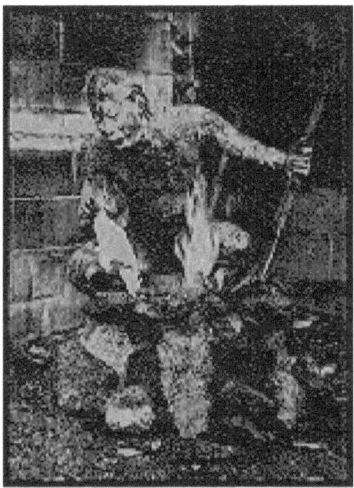

Pygoya, BC, 1985

I like watching people at art exhibition openings. I have had over a hundred receptions over decades as artist and also managed a retail gallery in Honolulu. These are some of my observations of folks in the social setting of the formal art opening.

The average time spent alone in front of a work of art is a couple seconds. If the spectator is moving from piece to piece with another person or group, dialogue about the work occurs, extending the time of the group stops in front a piece usually up to 30 seconds. After going through all the works, some will come back for a second and longer look at preferred works.

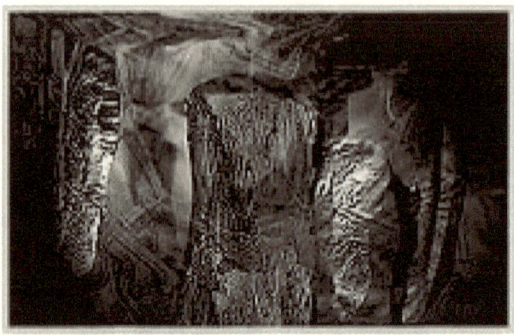

Tomb, digital

If there is food and drink provided the amount of time spent reviewing the works is reduced. It seems many spend more time around the refreshment table and punch bowl than actually pondering the artwork. Apparently for many invited to attend, the stomach is stronger than the heart. Of course this may not be such a bad thing, as any gallery director knows. Serving alcohol loosens the purse strings and opens the wallet. With booze the works start to look stronger and more vibrant. There is the increased chance that now some works seem "to speak" to the viewer, budgetary resistance can succumb to impulsive sales. Have a pretty salesperson "work the gallery floor" and ask guests about the work also assists sales volume.

Most naive viewers don't bother to look for more than a few seconds. Yet, they make a judgment of the depth of the work of art; deciding intuitively how much of their time is worth gazing at the painted surfaces on the wall. Ask what they think and many will declare, "I like it, but I don't know why." If they decide that they don't like it, usually they'll give a reason to defend their rejection of the art, such as, "I prefer something with more color."

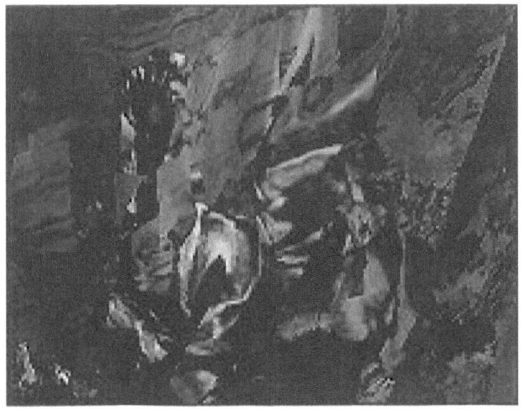

Implements, digital

Malcolm Gladwell in his new book, Blink, describes how we humans have two decision-making systems innately at work. One is a conscious effort to analyze to the hilt, factors that relate to a problem, in order to make a deliberate and rational selection among the multitude of possible solutions. This cautiousness may serve us well when there is adequate time to relegate to the situation. However sometimes, especially in "flight or fight" emergencies of our daily lives, we have to react on instinct - and after the fact judge if it is the correct action. This according to Gladwell is a programmed unconscious ability that has evolved to protect our survival as a species. We have sprung into action, without "thinking," for thousands of years.

I believe we naturally use a part of this unconscious system when we encounter artwork. I did some research on the art appreciation response a while ago (1980). I hypothesized that in just a few seconds our brain considers all these "aesthetic" factors and the sum result is our like or dislike response of the work as visual stimulus. I wrote of an evolution of mentality that today has many unconscious residual levels that influence our behavior without our conscious awareness. My reading of "Blink" (2005) now makes me consider a possible relationship between our cursory art judgment time and other human action that requires decision-making in 2 seconds. As I said earlier, the average time we look at art in galleries is a few seconds. Could it be that in a "blink" we judge whether an art object is critical to our personal welfare? Or is our natural capacity to appreciate art, without perceptual training through art education, obstructed by our natural defenses of scanning the environment and reducing attention towards anything benign and non-threatening?

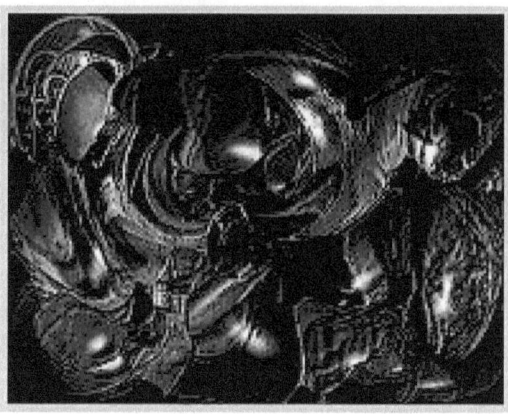

Armor, digital

I like to think that personal involvement with the right work of art leads to extended interest to the point of creating the desire to live with the piece (acquire it). For such a commitment to occur, perhaps there has to be a match similar to key and keyhole, of viewer and art object, that extends "seeing" beyond a blink, thereby opening up the portal to deeper meanings, emotions, and understanding of the self. If art can do that for us, it may indeed have survival value to us as a species through nourishment of spiritual health so lacking in today's world gone mad.

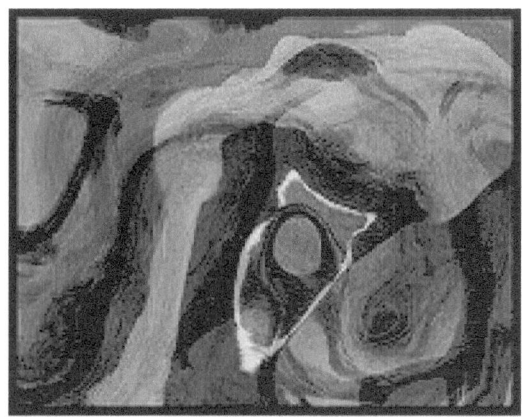

Artifacts, digital

My "Fifteen Minutes of Fame"

Honorary Professor Rodney E. J. Chang
(title bestowed by Shanghai University, College of Fine Arts, 1988)

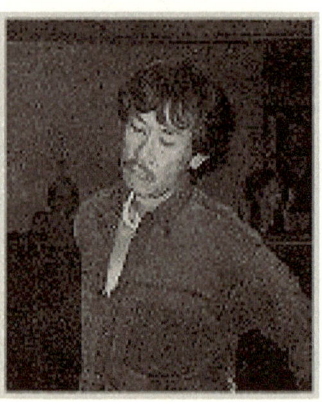

Sometimes fortune can still smile for one stuck in the wrong place - but the right time.

The year was 1985. I was the first local digital artist to show in a public exhibition space - the prestigious Honolulu Club. Imagine, the moment in a city when clubbers with drinks in their hands would be the first in that locale to witness framed-and-hung computer art. Way back at the start, in '85.

Pixels declared art! Over twenty years ago, before there was an Internet.

Now Honolulu ain't no New York, L.A., Chicago, Miami, or San Fran, so the partygoers at the artist's reception didn't know what to make or think of it. First looks didn't surface questions like "What is the artistic message?" similar to the search for the theme of a novel of fiction. No, instead the crowd's reaction to the images was "What is it?" or "What is it made of?" - curiosity that did not probe deep for aesthetic and philosophical substance.

My historic opening in this island state was basically shock and awe for a group of middle-age successful business types and socialites. That would have been enough satisfaction for me as the rebellious artist - tossing my brushes for a plastic mouse, and placing some pixels in everybody's face. But as fate would have it, this was nothing compared what this showing would net, for being "in the wrong place but the right time."

The newspaper review officially "published" the happening of this first digital art exhibition in Hawaii as not quite art. The reviewer wrote that the blocky tapestry appearance of the low-resolution pictures, daring to call itself "art" and heaven forbid, made with a machine, was not ready for prime time.

Luckily, it garnered quite a different reaction from two other attendees at the reception!

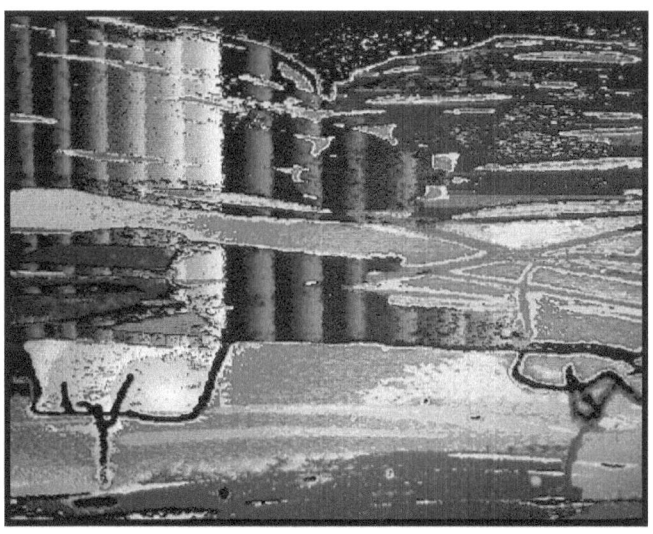

Next Century

Ji and Ida (she gave herself an English name) Jiang shook hands with the attending artist - me. They had recently come from China to study art here at the University of Hawaii. They were in their mid-twenties, traditionally schooled and accomplished in their painting craft, but unacquainted with postmodernism movements in America (Ida would come a long way; she is now an assistant professor in the art department of the local campus). They expressed to me that they had never seen anything like this in China. Imagine that, their eyes beamed, computer pictures as a new medium. As art! For Americans that's not much of an intellectual jump to make (but evidently not so for the elderly art columnist that reviewed the exhibit). There is a sense, and the resistance from conflicting interest groups within the art world, that everything is going digital. But for these two just out of communist China it was even more than that. They recognized the new medium imagery as a monumental leap that could forever change art as we know it. It was indeed new entities to their conceptual framework of just what is "art." Encountering their first digital art (even if it was in small town Honolulu -they were from the metropolis of Shanghai) made them interpret the new medium also as the moment's artistic symbol of Western intellectual (and creative) freedom. They were both anxious to share their new find with their fellow countrymen back home.

Luckily, they had the clout to do it. The two Chinese student artists turned out to be the young of families high up in the governing Communist Party. Members are networked. Ji (he later took the nickname "Lucky") and Ida felt the timing was right for the Chinese art world to be aware of the coming of digital fine art. There's nothing like the present when you feel behind. Any sample of the medium would do. Luckily, Lucky spotted and was charmed by my art at the Honolulu Club.

The timing was right, even if the artist knew himself to be born in the wrong place. I sold more when I had been painting, hand building ceramics, and casting bronze. But working (playing) on the computer back in 1984 was all that interested me at that moment in time. Computer graphics was seductive. It was a new medium in waiting to be developed by exploratory artists willing to take the career risks. It didn't (and still doesn't) sell well in the local tourist market.

Before I knew it the Jiangs had arranged a review of my work by the authorities, resulting in me receiving a formal invitation - no email back then - from the director of the Shanghai State Art Museum (no. 2 cultural institution after Beijing State Art Museum so they claimed). First floor, solo, space for 100 20x24 inch photographs at the museum (no good color printers yet; works shot off the monitor by a film camera and large prints developed at a custom photo lab), red carpet treatment.   Wow! It was the artist's dream of getting discovered, to take one's work out of the 'hood and hold it up to the world!

There was the government's stipulation that I conduct a 1-week workshop on "computer art" for China's art students - the gifted and selected were bussed in from around the nation for the course.   Rumors abounded among the students of how this American had milked new art from the computer.   Like I had cracked the code to generate art.   Others around the United States of course were also pioneering this effort.   For example, Laurence Gartel (NYC), Joan Truckenbrod (IL), Roz Dimon (NYC), Emily Young (OR), James Dowlen (CA), John Dunn (MI), Claude Horan (HI) and Daria Barclay (OR).   But luckily, for me, I was in the "right place at the right time" to catch the eye of the Asian dragon.

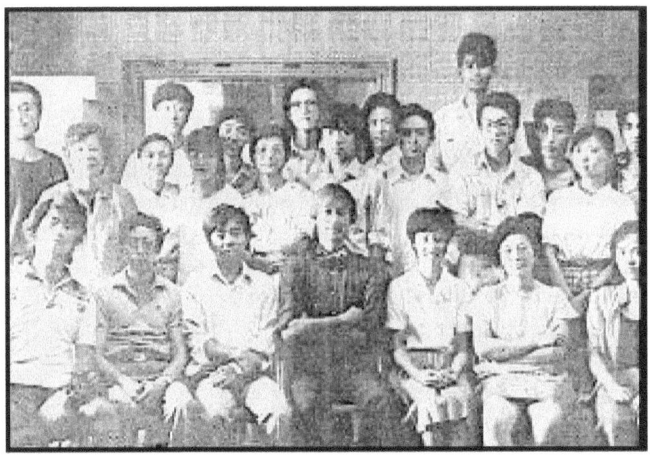

Rodney Chang, 1st row at center,
Shanghai University art classroom

I also had to donate the computer I used to make the artwork to Shanghai University's College of Fine Art. A security guard was posted outside the room every night to protect this cheap personal computer. I thought it was a joke but they took it quite seriously back then. He wore a sidearm. The U.S. government also took it seriously.   I had to clear the computer with the U.S. Department of Commerce. But there was no problem there; the Amiga 1000 made by Commodore had a measly 1-megabyte of operating ram (!) and a frugal 16-colors graphics card. It retailed for a grand. The creative challenge back then was attempting to make the blocky pixels look artsy. But the PC had enough firepower to catapult my work into a top museum of the most populous nation on the planet. The little computer-that-could landed me China's first digital art (solo) exhibition - also a first from the perspective of Chinese art history.

But maybe more importantly, five minutes of prime time evening news on the television.

I would watch that evening - back at the hotel (a soldier stationed at the elevator on each floor), flopped on the bed with a couple Chinese beers raging through my blood vessels - the TV news coverage of the museum exhibition opening. It included me cutting the red ribbon at the entryway with the city mayor at my side, moving my trusty mouse as I taught the class at the university on how to use "DigiPaint" (Electronic Arts, 1985 - their 1st product, art software, before they became the leader for producing digital games), and panning of the crowd gawking at my art. The exhibition was on the first floor, utilizing every gallery room to accommodate 100 framed, monitor-shot, digital creations. It was the first computer art for a nation of eyes - virgin to digital art, all glued to the television news - edited, presented, and sanctioned by the Chinese Communist Party. I had to pinch myself to confirm this was really happening.

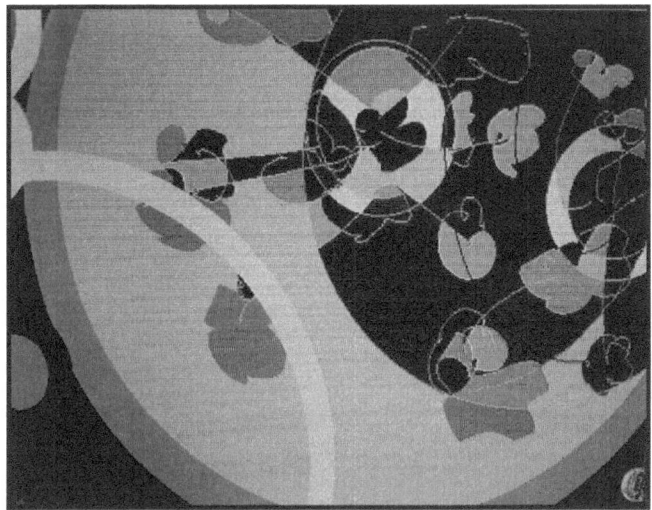

Geisha

At that time there was still just ONE television channel in the People's Republic of China, at least in Shanghai. At night when I walked the city streets and looked up into apartment windows, it seemed just about every family had their set turned on. So, lying there, drunken, and seeing myself on national TV news, I realized this really was a big deal. The captured TV audience was viewing their first computer art pictures in their respected national museum, told this is new art from America. The media coverage, including national cultural magazines, brought throngs to the 2-week exhibition.

At the opening, people stared at me as of I was from another planet. They leaned in close to inspect the horizontal lines of the low-resolution prints; the school children looked up at me in awe. We remained separated by different languages - and philosophies of art. Both sides remained in cultural shock. That peak experience and then witnessing my own mouse (and hand) move on a desktop and the resultant drawn line (jaggy/crude by today's standards) in front of millions of people with eyes glued to the tube, made me realize, lying there, at 40, and savoring the moment, that-

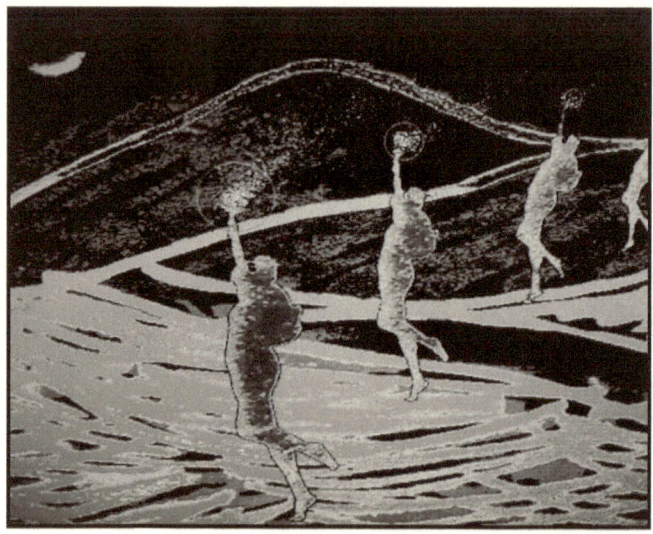

Spreading Liberty Abroad

This is how it feels to be granted Andy Warhol's "everybody has fifteen minutes of fame."

I remember reflecting no matter what else I achieved in this life as an artist, nothing would beat this.   Declaring and showing the new art form to a country with 1 billion eyeballs, scoring their top museum, receiving prime time 1-channel-only national TV, getting all the press (40 reporters), and then party and disco clubbing with a gorgeous opera singer that was assigned as my blind date by the state ...   I mean, how much better could it get? I realized then and there that this was going to be my life's "fifteen minutes of fame." What more is there to prove or do? I remember thinking to myself.

I would never have guessed the answer to be later building a virtual museum Web site, declaring a manifesto for the "Webism" art movement, and mounting an international collection of fine arts to perpetually display in online cyberspace. The building of a new global art culture. First online, then offline secondary influences. On the personal side, develop my work over the first two decades of PC development, then saddle up, ride out of town, and head east to Santa Fe with my art concoctions. I'm looking into opening a gallery there; maybe sell some snake oil on the side until I can make ends meet.

By 2006 the Web has grown to include a global swarm of digital artists' works, gracing limitless personal Web sites and precipitating the flocking into art groups. The technological means (global telecommunicating & networking) begets its own indigenous culture. From that innocent moment in 1988 of viewing primitive digital art in the Shanghai museum, millions today can key up digital (including mine) art by going to Google (or AbsoluteArts.com and LastPlace.com for that matter). No institutional vested interests can stop this avalanche of new art.

So fellow artists, you never know when opportunity will come knocking. Be prepared and be on the look out for it. I did. I was a serious artist stuck in a tourist trap and sheer luck still got me into a world-class international museum. Hey, it's great to be asked to give something back as an artist. Too bad not in my own back yard, so it may be time to hit the road. I travel to Santa Fe, New Mexico later this month for a personal appraisal of the "second largest art market in America." I'll give ya' all a report next month. Adiós, partners, and happy trails to you!

The "Pygoyan Gap"- Identified Mental Time Gap Between Naturalistic and Abstract Painting

April 10, 2008

For over 20 years as a digital artist I have avoided the genre of naturalistic imagery. *Why copy nature?* I thought to myself. Within the realm of the abstract was the challenge of starting from scratch. Through partnership with the personal computer was the opportunity to visualize the formerly unseen, to unearth new art, to discover new vision. It has been a marvelous life experience to remain loyal to this calling to explore the abstract that is capable of being visualized through the digital medium. I've had my work exhibited in museums, show opportunities scattered like buckshot over the decades. But sales remain minimal, not sufficient to earn me a living. But that was never the primary motivation. I felt confident profits would eventually come by pursuing excellence and discovery in the visual arts. By making history in the emerging art medium, integral to the new century's digital cultural revolution.

Turning 60 years of age triggered an immediate practical perspective on how to expend my present artistic life. Maybe, I thought, *I should start making what the market wants.* I always had confidence that if I *choose* to produce for its demand, I would be financially successful at it. Suddenly at this mature milestone in life, there emerged the desire to gain success in the only criteria of my art efforts that I considered myself yet a failure. To sell stuff. So I began a series of works with such an intent- to not just prove to myself that my works can be financially successful, but also to those around me who viewed me as a "starving artist" fanatic, fortunate to be buffered from the demands of real life by my day job as a dentist.

My new works start with my photographs of beautiful Hawaii that are infused with personal expression through digital photo manipulation, and then finally materialized as "output," in the form of oil-on-canvas paintings. It was refreshing to discover that I do *like* these realistic landscapes as much as I like my routine abstract work. I felt good about the results and comfortable with myself. I'm so excited about this direction of my art that I now contemplate publishing another art book of my works, this one including "Nature" and "Abstract" in the titling.

The start of my current digital nature series began with the profit motive. But doing the lifelong rejected, the disregarded, and the undesirable has unexpectedly revealed new art psychological insight to me!

I have commissioned painters to work for me since 1985. Completed landscape oil paintings arrive in email to gain approval for shipping. I have been showing them to people around me. The subjects as experimental observers provide me subjective responses to the new visual stimuli (artworks). Those immediately available happen to be relatives and dental patients. Through these initial and impromptu reactions, I have discovered the following about ourselves as a species-

For such attractive realistic landscape paintings, there is an INSTANT REACTION of art appreciation. It is as if something in the psyche is triggered. There is no hesitation of response. The results so far have been as predictable as winning in poker with a loaded (card) deck. Everybody *loves* my "new work." I get responses like "Now *this* is what I like;" "This is your best work ever!" Huh?

Then a predictable second response follows, as captured in the remark, "It looks so realistic that it *must have* taken you a *long* time to complete." This is an indirect prying way to ask, "So *how painstakingly long* did it take to paint?"

I have always known that fine craftsmanship necessitating tedious labor contributes to appreciation of art-making results. To *do the time* to craft well helps sell the work. It seems collectors like to own art that was arduous to construct. No pain, no gain. In essence they are paying not only for the piece, but also for the artist's time and tedious labor to produce the product. Maybe this is one reason digital art is a tough sell. It seems too easy to make. I've personally adjusted to this prejudice towards the dubious art medium by dubbing myself a "digital painting designer," as a replacement for my former label of "digital artist." I continue to prefer spending my creative time with inspiration for the sake of aesthetic exploration. It is not selfishness with my creative time but my methodology for enhanced efficiency and increased production, as expected of an artist using high technology. I turn over the captured digital imagery to professional painters, astute in replicating what's captured in my digital visual data. I pay for their labor to output my digital visions. The collaboration materializes my virtual art for the brick n' mortar world of objects, be it a painting, print, or sculpture.

But what's new that I have discovered, now dabbling in landscape realism, is that there is a momentary pause of the viewer when looking at the abstract that isn't present when peering at the realistic landscape artwork. The time lapse of silence, before the utterance of a personal judgment, can be a mere second but as long as a few more seconds. Call it introspection. But I hypothesize that it is a mental confrontation with the unknown, a sudden challenge to have to decipher "What is it?" before the mind can then judge "Do I like it?" These two imperative internal questions must be answered before the mind can leap to "Do I want to live with it?" which in turn can lead to the conclusive "I want to buy it!"

Why this gap of response –which I hereby dub the *Pygoyan gap* – in comparative viewer response time between the landscape and the abstract? Here's my take on this identified phenomenon in art perception and appreciation:

We as humans have a built-in conditioning to appreciate naturalistic artwork. We have evolved over millions of years in an environment and continue to live in nature. Those who reside in a big city environment yearn for a vacation in "the country." It's instinctive. Might not our affinity for naturalistic artwork be, dare I say, inherited? Genetic? Maybe a part of what the great psychologist Carl Jung calls our shared "universal consciousness?" With my new awareness of the existence of the *Pygoyan gap*, I now reconsider what it means when someone defensively says, "I *know* what I like" while viewing art that is dumbfounding. I wonder if that person's sense of artistic taste is *derived* and actually quite impersonal, an artistic bias embedded in the origin of the species.

All trained artists know that the building blocks of naturalistic imagery are hidden abstract forms. For example a mountain can have a spherical form, a leaf a triangular shape. A massive tree trunk's visual infrastructure is an upright rectangle. Maybe looking at abstract work is not natural to our eyes. We are not adapted to *seeing* the underpinnings of nature. But dedicated looking by educating the eye through due diligence in practice and extended exposure to the arts can teach appreciation of such hidden elements of natural representation.

But for most, the lay "masses," representational artwork provides *instant gratification.* That potentially skews sales and higher returns for realistic art. There is no injustice here against abstract art. It's just the nature of the beast.

A parting thought – what if I replace the idyllic paradisiacal landscape with a painting of less inviting scenery, such as the harsh southeastern New Mexican desert? Would this retard or even cancel out the *Pygoyan gap* effect? Hmm, I wonder...

This scientific curiosity may indeed lead to an intentionally ugly or menacing landscape series, definitely retarding or even canceling out its profitability. (Unless one loves the broiling inhospitable desert, crawling with scorpions, tarantulas, and rattlesnakes.) Hmmm, inspiring thought to provoke me to later divorce my effort in amiable landscape imagery comfortably rooted in Romanticism, and move on.

Side note: "Creativity" is the correlating of two or more things when they have never been associated before. Try it. Fill in the blanks: _____ and _____ can make/improve/ _____ by _____; or, _____ is like _____ because... Getting into realistic landscapes besides my regular abstract work did stir up the creative notion of the *Pygoyan gap.*

Life lesson: As a lifelong abstractionist, working on realistic landscapes provided an experimental "confounding variable" that unexpectedly made my regular abstract work the "control group." This provided heuristic insight that led to personal artistic growth. Moral: Don't be afraid to explore outside your self-imposed boundaries!

Rodney E. J. Chang

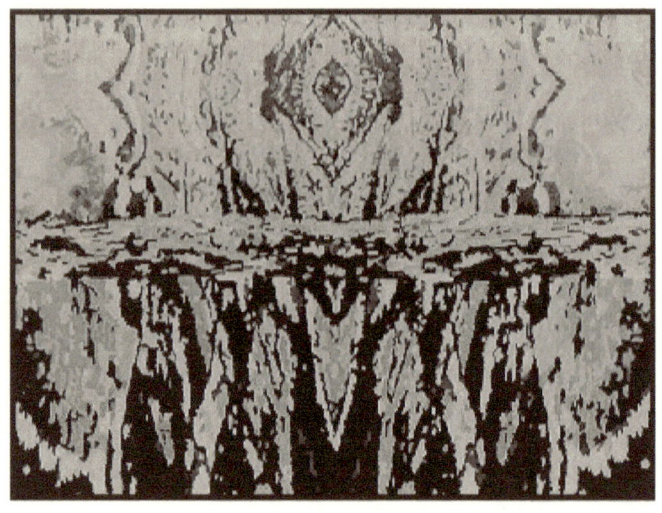

Abstract, 1985

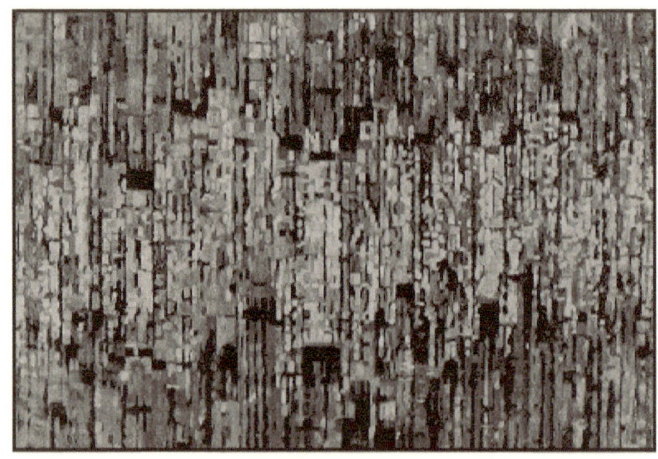

Abstract, 1991

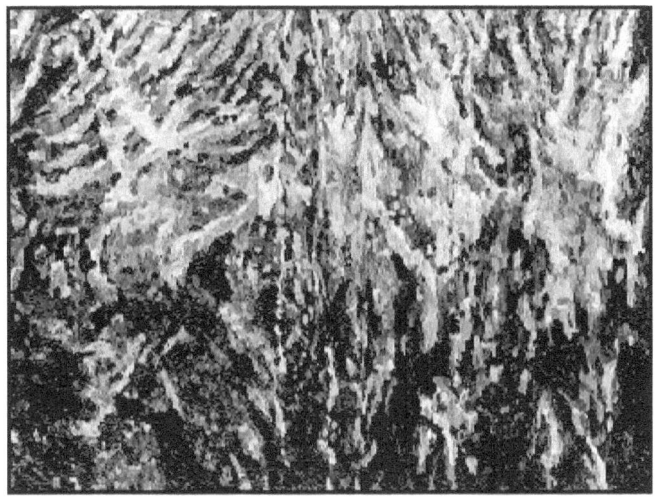

Abstract, 1995

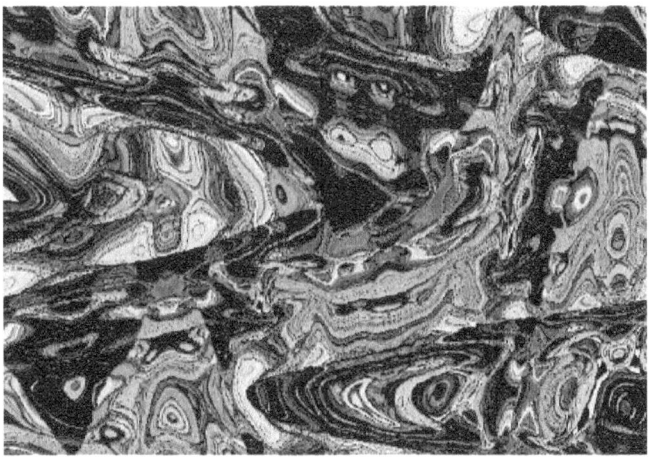

Abstract, 2000

Rodney E. J. Chang

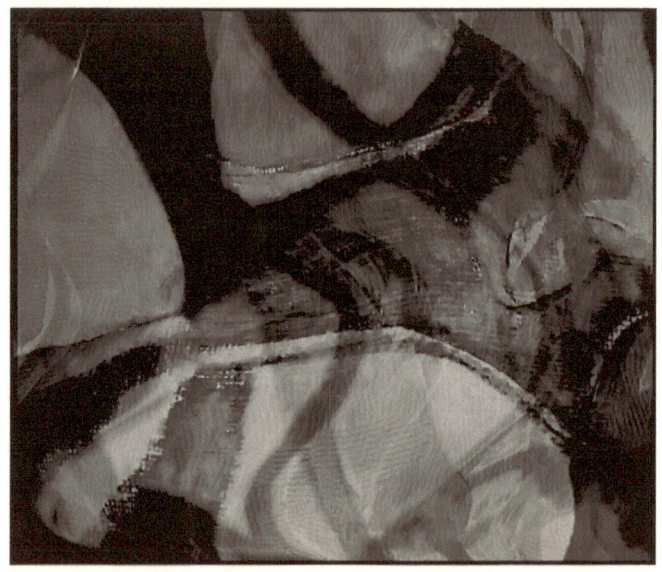

Abstract, 2007

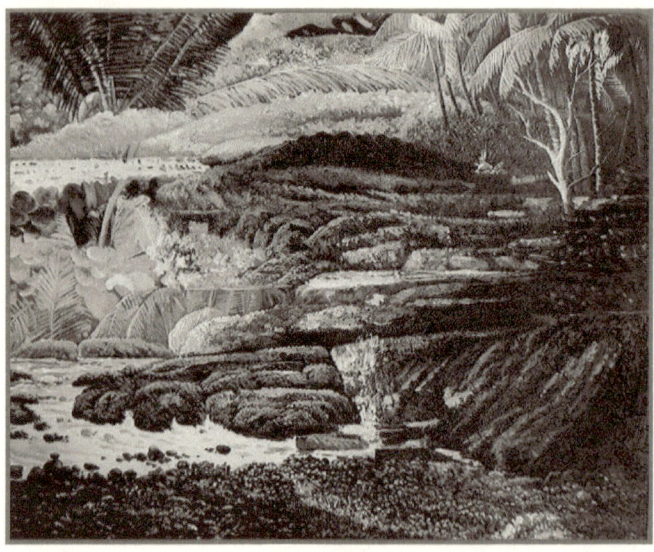

Landscape, 2008

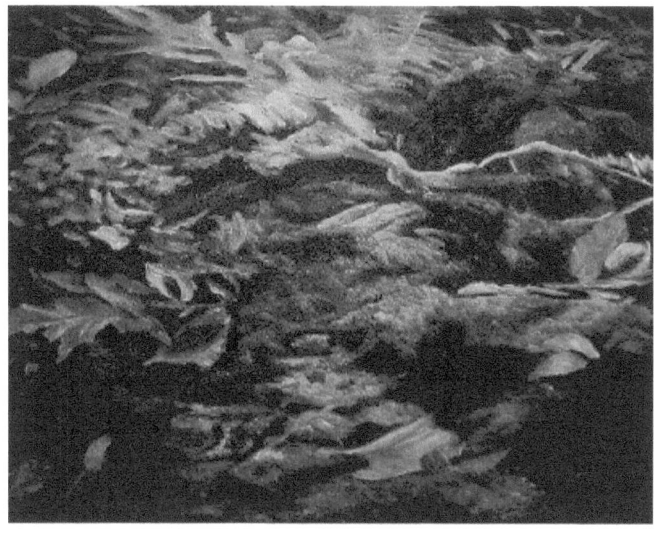

Landscape, 2008

Cerebral Conflict in Abstract Art Perception

April 15, 2008

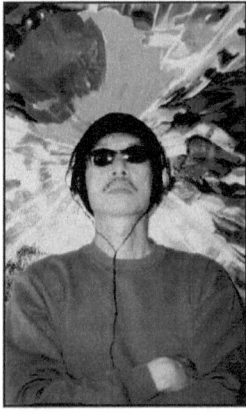

Rodney Pygoya Chang, M.A., MS.Ed., Ph.D.*

I previously identified a difference in reaction time between realistic landscape and abstract art. I hypothesized that this *Pygoyan Gap* is the result of comparing naturalistic scenery in which we have adapted to over the ages, with abstract imagery, not overtly obvious in our naturalistic environment. I now believe there is another factor that retards the reaction time of appreciating (or disliking) an abstract work of art when we confront it, as in a gallery setting.

We react to the realistic landscape painting on a *visceral* level. This mental response comes from the part of the brain that evokes the sense of pleasure. A rendered idyllic landscape does not demand that the viewer *solve* anything. The artist in fact enhances the real world scene to beautify it, making it more glorious than it appears in the physical world.

For example, the painter can increase lushness by adding richer greens to the trees and ground and by using more brilliant reds and yellows for the fields of flowers. All landscape paintings also position elements in the work, such as trees, mountain, ocean, and clouds, to be spatially arranged for perfect visual balance. A less artistic but related visual act is for a tourist to walk about to find the best viewpoint for taking a souvenir photograph of a picturesque place. Likewise, a painter on location will position his easel and self from a vantage point in his or her judgment best suited to capture its beauty.

In these ways, the artist makes the natural scene his or her own. The embellishments make the scene now the artist's subjective statement about the real world location. In other words, the physical scene in now modified with the artist's emotions and cosmetic augmentations and thereby elevated to a categorical "work of art."

Unlike the completely visceral reaction to a pastoral painted scene, looking at abstract art is more complex. Although the mind reacts to the beautifying elements of the work, such as balance of composition and color harmony of the overall piece, it is confused by the lack of obvious subject matter (such as depicted/provided by realistic landscape artwork).

Another part of the brain must be brought into action in order to *judge* the affective quality of the work. The left hemisphere comes into play to handle the required *problem solving*. The person unconsciously asks, "What is it?" besides "Do I like it?" when viewing the exhibited artwork. The first question must be answered before the second can be addressed. Adding this analytical component to the enjoyment response of looking at abstract art *lengthens* the reaction time in the judgment of whether or not one likes/appreciates a specific work of art.

There is also the *precondition* of expecting to experience pleasure when looking at art. We go to gallery openings with a *hedonistic* frame of mind, anticipating "warm fuzzies" (good feelings) when engaging the displayed art. A show of Romantic landscapes doesn't disappoint. An exhibit of abstruse shapes and exotic forms might challenge the intellect, but confound or even disrupt the more primal response of pleasure.

Artists can take into consideration these two different cerebral activities in spectators of art. For an almost reflexive pleasurable reaction to a landscape painting, they should not include any object that might raise questions about the content.

For example in a glorious sunset desert scene, do not add a cattle skull in the foreground. This might suggest to the viewer that the work includes a symbolic metaphor of death; that the artist might be making a statement other than just glorifying the attractiveness of a place.

For the abstractionist, naturalistic setting or background for featured geometric forms can strengthen the pleasure reaction,especially if strong colors and compositional layout lead the viewer to perceive the naturalistic setting first, then only secondarily notice the abstract components of the piece, leading to subsequent contemplation. To create such works, computer graphic software is a *better tool* than the brush. Digital 3-dimensional forms use minute and indiscernible geometric shapes as building blocks for the overall complex forms that we perceive. The artist, like myself, can select to permit the underlying geometric construction of the work to manifest itself as part of the character and style of the visualized work. For example, review the sample artwork, below and on the right.

Interestingly, elementary children's art is based upon geometric forms to represent real world things. For example, the circle is used as the Sun or human face, the triangle represents a house's roof, and the square becomes the house's living space and windows. You might say that the child's mind is the first simplistic pictorial generator, similar to the graphic capability of 1970s PCs (like the IBM XT and 64K Atari). Although the child seems to instinctively understand the connection between basic geometric shapes and objects of their environment, when they become adults that awareness is lost by most. Many seniors in retirement go to art classes and learn to draw by becoming familiar with the geometric nature of complex forms. Most don't think or remember far back enough to realize that they naturally possessed this understanding before. Picasso was astute in studying children's art to inspire primal basic forms to power his bizarre yet radically innovative portrayal of the human figure.

Making art that made the invisible visible helped form the Cubism movement.

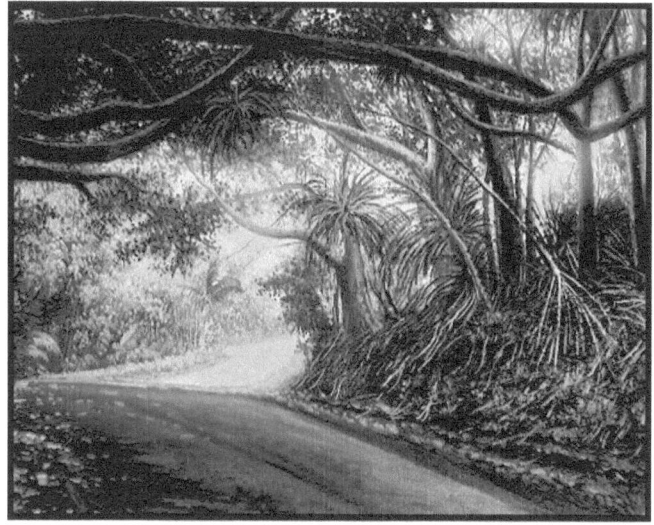

Landscape

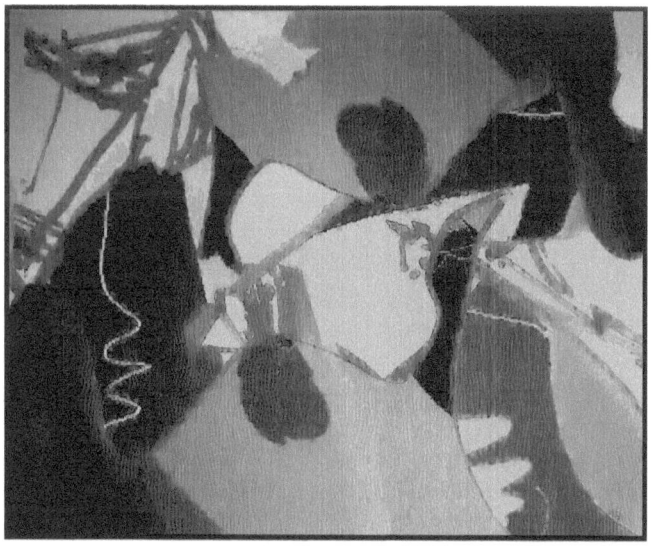

Abstract

Rodney E. J. Chang

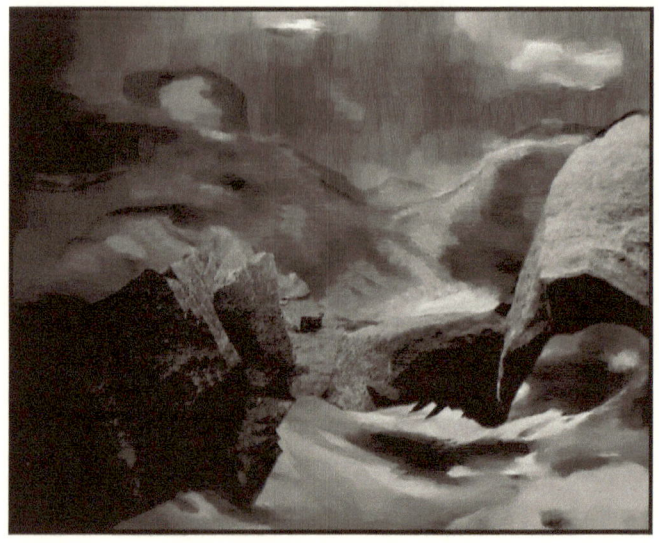

Abstract forms in landscape setting

The Master's Touch

Main Street, a digital dead end
(See artwork below)
By Rodney Pygoya Chang, digital painting designer
February 28, 2008

Not many critics can criticize the craftsmanship of the oil on canvas painting entitled "Main Street." I, the "creator" of the piece, had it executed with the finest traditions of photo-realism in mind and in intent. Truth to what was captured by the camera was strictly adhered to. Note the piece of litter on the left curve of the street (below corner of building in left foreground). It's in the artist's opinion a fine documentary of life, as it now exits, in Pahoa town on the Big Island of Hawaii.

But was the creation of a masterful depiction of this town scene the objective for undertaking this work? Not by a long shot. Was it to display my talent as a painter of realism? Not so. In fact, like the kid being judged for worthiness to get a gift from Santa in the film, "The Polar Express," begs, "I didn't do it!" (Bad behavior), I didn't "paint" the picture. But I claim authorship. Through the stewardship of my creative process the world is rewarded another great artwork. I don't literally have to "do it" in my formulated creative process to wean fine arts from the digital realm.

Here's how I do "do" it. The scene was captured with a digital camera as I rode in a car through town. Then I had fun "photo-manipulating" the scene until it echoed my sentiments, felt frozen forever in time, and elicited a sense of nostalgia for the disappearing of Small Town America (due to the changing global economy). Taking out the specifics of time of day, specific place, and the bright and gaudy colors of this funky tourist street, I deemed the result successful in the creation of a generic American scene, quickly becoming extinct in the 21st century.

Ok, so much for the romantic reason and attraction others have for this work of art. Now how about fine art issues, such as turning over a photograph to somebody to paint as collaborator? For a buck?

Here's the way I see it. I prefer to do my own thing, adhere to the digital abstract where I'm in complete control. No leaning on Mother Nature to provide me subject matter that assists others to understand. Pure integration of color, shapes, forms, space, and light, albeit of the digital kind, not paints on a tangible surface. Like classical music the beauty is captured in the interplay of such fundamental compositional elements. No need for lyrics, or here, subject matter as a guiding narrative.

Here's the point, the true reason why this realistic painting breaks new ground. Heaven knows so many other works have been rendered at this level of photographic realism. So that's not the criteria as far as I am concerned that determines its aesthetic worth. (Nice picture, though, quite soothing and nostalgic.) But the artistic "statement" is this - through digital tools, such a work can be materialized effortlessly. I click; I push and pull, collage in Photoshop, then farm out the digital file to be rendered by a "human printer." Without a digital "blue print" file the painting craftsperson wouldn't have anything to "copy." The skill level of my staff is so masterful that the reproduction (the oil on canvas) is identical to the original digital image. Well, almost.

This particular piece does have another innovative perspective. I choose to include the dashboard of the old car to defy formal standards of portraying the classical landscape. The viewer rides along in the automobile, eliciting both a sense of transience as well as unimportance of the moment. This isn't a heroic moment like the Marines planting the flag at Iwo Jima. Nah, just a tourist passing through town, taking a "quickie" snapshot to record this moment of his trip. (At that moment, little did I know it would become this famous "painting.") This attempt to capture an insignificant or mundane moment makes the painting kindred to the earlier Pop Art movement.

Now in my process I then take it to the professional print shop, have the painting redigitalized to a massive 100+-megabyte size digital file. This enables me to produce huge 40x50 inch Giclee prints. By magnifying the scale I then can exhibit "Main Street" at a size much larger than my itty-bitty 17-inch monitor. In a lush and expensive looking frame, I then welcome the digital simulation of reality (Nature), veiled as a painted imitation, to the brick and mortar world where the apartment wall, my couch, and I exist.

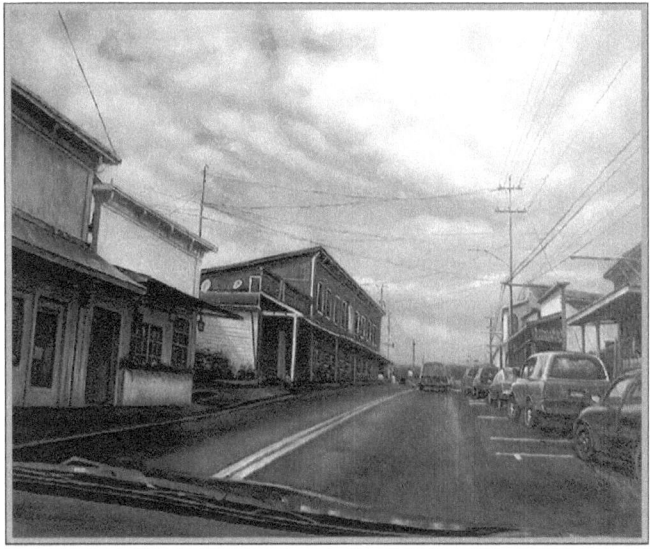

Main Street - Pygoya, 2008

FINALLY, Validation via Art Historian

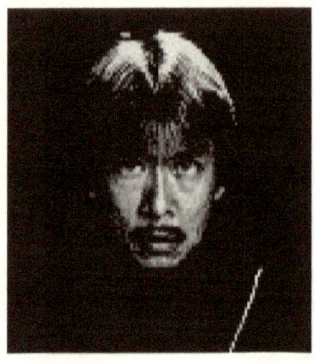

Rodney Pygoya Chang, M.A., Ph.D.

On a remote Pacific island distant from Mainstream Art
May 4, 2008

A satisfying feeling of validation has been bestowed to me. Ingrid Kamerbeek, art colleague on the other side of the planet, sent good news to me today by email. If not for her diligent monitoring of the infinite art cyberspace of the Internet, I would probably never have known what had occurred in February of this year. What could be so wonderful to make me feel like Clint Eastward, with someone who did "make my day?" In Dallas-Ft. Worth, Texas, at the 96th annual conference of the national College Art Association, was a formal presentation of my *creative process*! By association and examples to illustrate the speaker's description of my art making methodology, my art had to have been displayed through electronic projection. This would also validate the artist's works, as no creative process would get profiled at such a prestigious event without the art being judged to be great (or at least successful and original) as product. The audience was distinguished college art instructors and professors of American universities and colleges.

As one of five presentations on innovation in contemporary printmaking, Monica Kjellmann-Chapin, professor of art history, presented *Reproduction on Reverse: The Paradoxical Production of Pygoya*. I have not read the lecture notes, as it is not available on the Internet. But from the title, I gather that it is about my process of "digital painting design." It entails a shocking, for most traditionalists, reversal of values in regards to art medium and the intent of the artist. I work digitally to design and produce an original oil-on-canvas painting. But the painting is only an intermediary step to get to the final product, which is an edition of archival quality digital giclee prints-on-canvas. After the creation of the edition, the painting can be disposed or dumped as a collectible. Bottom line, the painting is a reproduction of the original digital image! Although the handcrafted work is true to the original digital picture, now the print edition is a direct descendent of a medium accepted as "fine art." Mind games yes, strange if not weird but logical - for an art market still stuck in the past century.

It is marvelous to know I have made a dent in the ivory tower of art academia. After toiling, financially sacrificing, and being ignored for over two decades (including the local University of Hawaii art department and island art museums), it's nice – especially as a Rodney (as in Dangerfield)- to get some "respect." I feel like the load (of self doubt and art medium prejudice) to prove myself has been lifted from my shoulders this fine day in Paradise. To have a professor of art history proclaim one's creative process and thoughts as significant to the culture-at-large, in front of a distinguished audience of college art professors, is so much more satisfying than selling the stuff. I always, however, did believe that if one rises to fame as explorer of the aesthetic process (Ph.D., Art Psychology), one's output – even the inferior works, would be coveted as collectibles. In other words, then even the inferior/ failures/crap sells along with the masterpieces. What a wonderful – and profitable- day that would be. The studio rent would always get paid!

From the perspective of economics, my art process is an aesthetic manifestation of the new global economy. It's cost effective for my digital creations to be *outsourced* for skilled human labor. Then the high quality *oil imports* are scanned, number crunched back into a data pool of 1's and 0's, as preparation to be remate-rialized to complete their final destination - as digital prints. In essence, in this high tech-Internet cultural climate, the painting in my art process is sandwiched between digital means of personal expression.

Academic discovery and notice of my life's work in art is a win for all digital artists. It is an incremental contribution to the inte-gration of digital art-making tools with the other more traditional means of visual human expression.

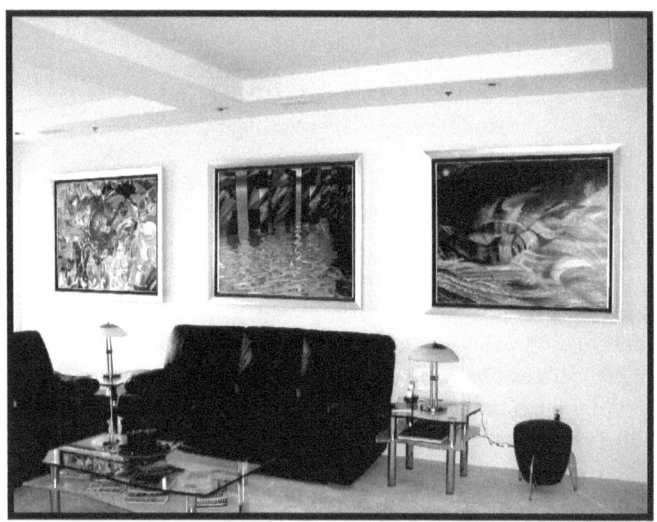

Reproductions or originals?
Photo courtesy of Richard & Sylvia Gessler, collectors

The lecture was one of five for the symposium session entitled –
The Vernacular Print in Contemporary Art, chaired by Beauvais Lyons
of the University of Tennessee
Thursday, February 21, 2008 2:30 PM–5:00 PM
Lone Star Ballroom A4, 2nd Floor, Adam's Mark Hotel

COLLEGE ART ASSOCIATION
275 Seventh Avenue, 18th Floor
New York, NY 10001
T: 212-691-1051 | F: 212-627-2381

The College Art Association supports all practitioners and interpreters of visual art and culture, including artists and scholars, who join together to cultivate the ongoing understanding of art as a fundamental form of human expression. Representing its members' professional needs, CAA is committed to the highest professional and ethical standards of scholarship, creativity, connoisseurship, criticism, and teaching.

Derivativism
-Sandwiching oils between digital buns

Rodney Pygoya Chang, Ph.D. (Art Psychology)
May 27, 2008

There is a difference in my creative art process between "copy" and "replication." Let me explain. As artist I start off with digital tools, use oil paints as an intermediate step, then end up with a digital derived final product. So how does this compare and differ from the commonplace procedure of reproducing paintings by copyists? I'll try to clarify so here goes-

I started off in painting and sculpture, earning a master's degree in Studio Art (Northern Illinois University, 1975). This developed an affinity as well as artistic sensitivity for the expressive powers of the paint medium. But with the introduction of the personal computer (PC graphics) in the 80s, I decided to emerge along with it as digital artist. I abandoned my paint tubes and brushes. In the beginning I was a purist, never scanning or importing photographs (of course back then there was no digital camera). I took pride in starting with clusters of pixels on an otherwise blank monitor screen. But times have changed and my attitude and approach has evolved along with the medium. My work now is truly "multi-media" or as they said before, "mixed media." I am now free to use whatever resources are available to make innovative imagery.

Which brings me to the issue of "original" and "reproduction." How do these terms relate to my idiosyncratic approach to producing art?

Other artists who create a painting may have their work later duplicated by another individual, whether willingly or not. The first painted image is the "original" and the subsequent effort(s) is a "copy." In this case the medium is the same. Both are paint on canvas. Today because of economics and the advancement of technology, the original can also be "duplicated" through digital photography and digital printmaking. Archival quality print editions called "Giclees" can be offered at a more affordable price to many collectors instead of just one. The original painting so popularized by the multitude of identical print imagery thereby also appreciates in value, or price.

My art making process differs. I start off with a completed digital image on the computer monitor display. My "original" is represented virtually by photons of light called pixels that are directed in visual attributes by computer data stored as files. My "original" is actually a bunch of numbers in a computer database. Its display as a picture on the screen is merely temporary. When the image file is closed or the computer turned off, there is no picture. There is no visual/visible art. In the "early days" my digital art was either printed or photographed off the monitor. The latter method was used to frame hardcopy prints for my 1988 solo exhibition at the Shanghai Art Museum. It was by the way, the first digital art exhibition in China, thereby making *Chinese* art history.

But from this standard way of capturing the digital image and being able to touch it, frame it, and display it, my work has evolved. Maybe it was because of my earlier studio work in painting and drawing at Northern Illinois. Besides, after remaining the purist as a digital artist, it started to feel stale. I wanted to experiment outside of conventional digital imagery. Supported by an aesthetic theory and philosophy through years of exploring the psychology of art, I moved on to develop my systems approach that incorporated other media besides the digital. My work also embraced a team approach, with me as primary artist and image-making visionary.

I either start from scratch in front of the monitor with a blinking light cursor waiting to be led. Or I can load into ram memory a former digital image and take it further or into a new direction. Alternately I can use my professional photography skills and import imagery from my digital camera. After manipulation with mixed bag of graphic software, I arrive with an image that I judge with confidence in having made the transformation from merely "computer graphics" to literally fine art. I go ahead and "save" a work of art, still in its initial, or "original" state and form.

Somewhere over the decades I evaluated a purely digital image to still be too machine-like, too technically perfect to achieve my specific goal as a digital artist. I aspire to achieve works that convincingly simulate the appearance of paintings manually produced on canvas. So in order to "soften" the unyielding calculated imagery generated through the dictation of mathematical functions, I farm out my digital pictures to be actually painted-by-hand. Selected collaborators who are masters in their craft execute the task. Remember that in my case the digital image is the original. Therefore the subsequent painting cannot be a "copy," as this term requires the existence of an actual painting. So just what is the painting of a digital image, for the role that it performs in my creative process?

It is a "replication" of the digital image. It is also, however, transient like the original. The digital image disappears when the file is closed. The knock off painting is merely a means to an end. As good as the craftsman is in replicating the digital "blueprint," there is subtle variation from the original digital that cannot be avoided. Such "error" in the translation between media is intentionally added by me, the "digital painting designer." For one thing we are using a different media to transpose the digital. The computer picture is *projected* dots of light into the human retina. Color and form of a painting are light waves *reflected* off opaque surfaces (of paint and canvas). One image is made of pixels of light, the other of paint. Then there is human error that cannot be avoided, as the infinite amount of visual information of a detailed digital image cannot be completely captured by the limits of both the paint medium as well as the accuracy and skill of the individual artisan. The human as computer printer is imperfect. As I said before, this margin of error in the replication process is not only anticipated but also desired. Because of such deviance the high-tech, hard edge look of the digital imagery can be "cut" or reduced, giving the secondary image a hands-on feel and appearance. Through the hands of humans my digital picture is "softened" and soothed. By using the limitation of the paint medium, my simulated digital "paintings" are more convincingly perceived as paint.

But the painting produced from the digital picture is not the end of my process. The object is digitally photographed, ironically converting the picture back to pixels. After personally enhancing the captured image with software, printing test prints to proof and doing the subsequent adjustments, this final digital file of the original digital image is offered as a limited edition Giclee print. I define the print as "derivative" of the whole process. I dub it "derivative" art and my artistic intent, process and final imagery as the new art of "Derivativism."

To summarize, other artists have paintings "copied" or "reproduced." I instead create a digital image; have it "replicated" in order to "derive" a final digital (once again) print. It can be tossed (in 2006 I literally destroyed 175 canvas paintings), or sold (they *are* beautiful and masterfully crafted) to an admirer. Or, as documentary of my long-term process leading to an extensive series of print editions, the intermediary paintings could be exhibited in a hall of their own. In such a paradoxical way would they compliment as well as elevate an audience's appreciation of the monumentally scaled (40"x50") derivative print collection. The Giclees would *be* the featured works, installed as the main exhibition of my future digital art museum.

Everybody expects artwork to be signed. So, you may ask, how is the art signed? I back off as Rodney Chang, multi-media conceptual artist. Instead I sign "Pygoya" for the team of Pygoya Productions.

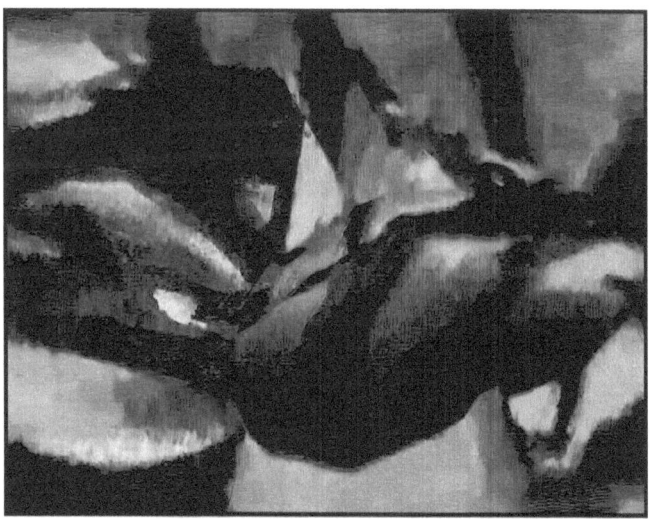

Sailing in Cyberspace, 2003   - original digital

Rodney E. J. Chang

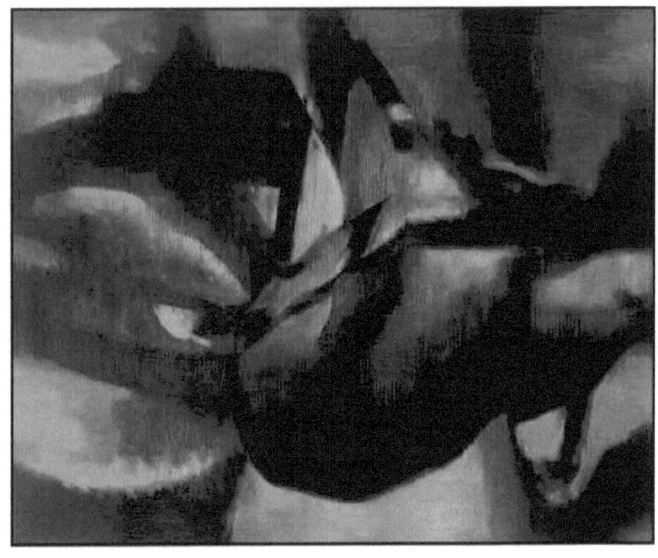

Sailing in Cyberspace, 2003 - oil painting

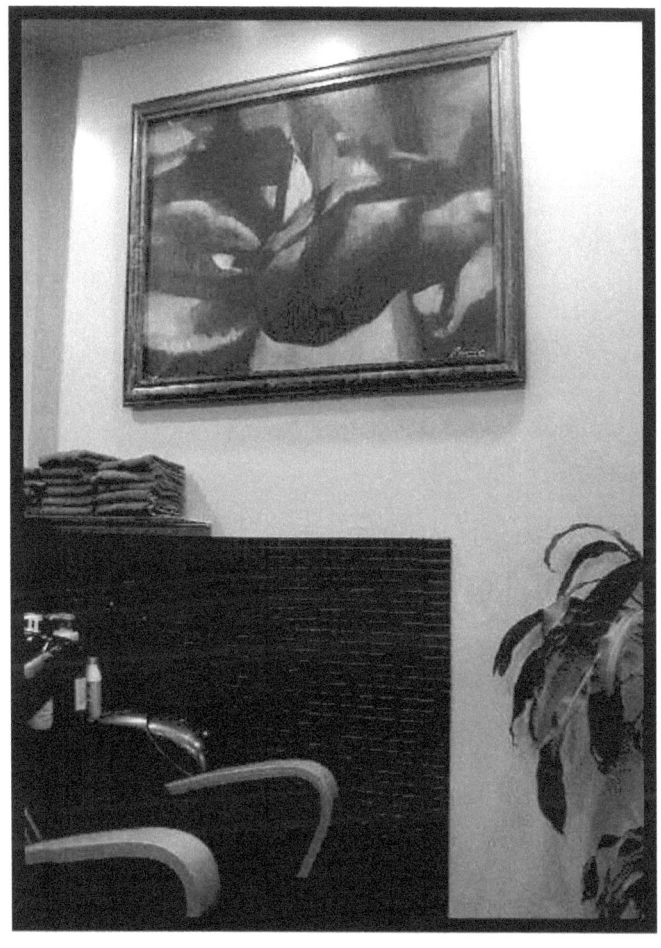

Sailing in Cyberspace, 2003 - 40" x 50" Giclee canvas print
Photograph courtesy, V Salon, Manhattan, New York City, NY

Rodney E. J. Chang

Appendix

Appendix 1

This is the original text that was used to create the description of the book's contents for its back cover. The unedited writing is included here as it provides more information about the artist's process than does the version on the cover, significantly reduced in length to accomodate cover design.

Introduction

Using art psychology, the Internet, and a systems approach that embraces digital media and collaboration, Dr. Rodney Chang has, over a lifetime, developed his idiosyncratic methodology of deriving innovative as well as relevant contemporary art for the dawn of the 21st Century.

While in graduate art school in Chicago, he remembers a crucial moment in his fledging art career. During a painting class, he asked his painting professor what she thought about some of the aesthetic concepts in Rudolf Arnheim's <u>Art and Visual Perception</u> (U. of California Press, Berkeley and Los Angeles, 1969). The instructor obviously never heard of it and defensively blurted out, "STOP thinking so much and work harder on your painting ability - if you ever expect to graduate!" It was at that moment that Chang realized his path for a future life of art exploration, an inquisition into the eternal question, "What is Art?," lied outside the conventional philosophy that is embedded in the educational process of the artist.

After graduating with a Masters in Studio Art, Chang became a student of psychology, moving up the ranks from Associate, Bachelor, Masters degrees to the final Doctor of Philosophy in Art Psychology. Yet landing a teaching position was not the goal of all this academic rigor, uncommon for an artist. The motivation remained throughout to gain a broad range understanding of the process of creativity and its influence on the resultant product called "art." The hypothesis was drawn that the secret to finding a key to discovering and producing masterpieces lay within the human mind – or thinking- itself.

After over ten years of research and experimentation, the artist-psychologist hit the ground running, armed with his aesthetic perceptual formula that reduced "art appreciation" of an audience to a mathematical equation. Did it work? Did it help spin art materials into golden works of art? The working artist has published full color art books of his efforts, the "results" of his analytical approach to the making of original art. As for the level of his success, you be the judge. Go to Google.com and key in "Pygoya cyberpaintings." Better yet order the book by writing – Creative Frontiers International, Inc., 2119 N. King St., Honolulu, HI 96819 or go to Truly Virtual Web Art Museum at Lastplace.com. Limited edition archival prints that are exhibited in his Honolulu gallery are available for collectors at www. PygoyaGallery.com.

The range of subject matter is incredible – if not incredulous. Chang dives into abstracts, photo-realism landscapes, sculpture, ceramics, mixed media and even UFO theme art. He tackles thorny philosophical questions such as if digital imagery really is "fine art" and how the definition of "original" and "copy" are obsolete in the new digital age of high technology and the Internet.

What this book consists of are selections of the artist-psychologist journal (or "diary" if you prefer) that documents Chang's mental journey as he attempts to understand where his developing ideas and understanding of the nature of art are taking his constantly evolving art. The hope is that other professional artists and art students will gain some insight about the creative process and how it can be applicable to their own personal growth and artwork. This publication also functions as documentation of the life work of Chang, whose worth as an artist – and aesthetic psychologist – cannot completely be appreciated by merely looking at his artwork. Understanding the psychology behind the works enriches the experience of viewing his art.

Appendix 2

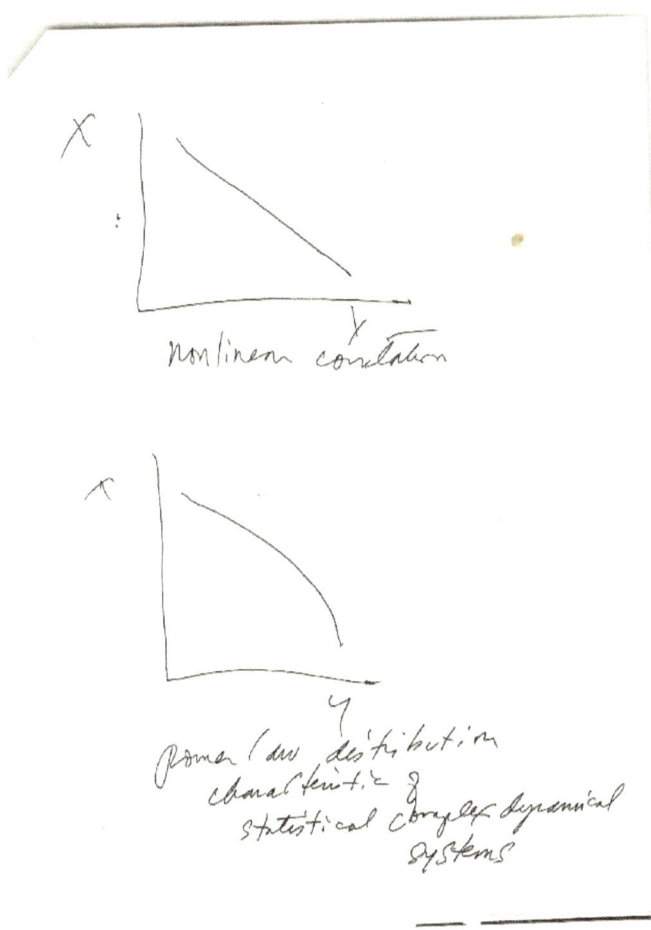

Figure 1 - Power law distribution characteristic of statistical
complex dynamical systems
(see p. 48 *The Chaotic Existence of the Computer Artist*)

Rodney E. J. Chang

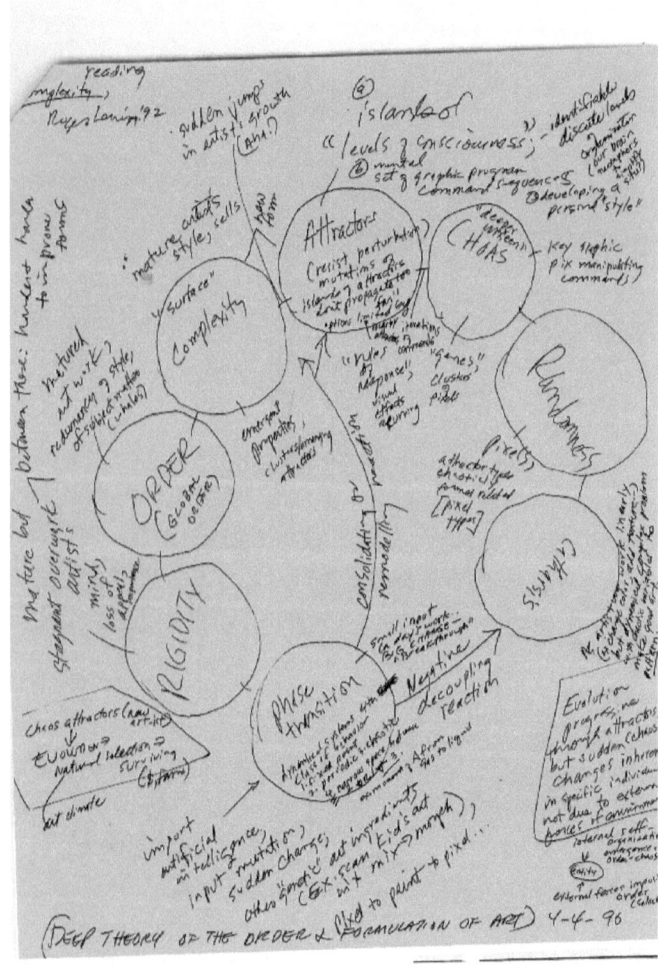

Figure 2 - Pygoya's theory of the order and formulation of art
(see p. 48 *The Chaotic Existence of the Computer Artist*)

Notes